Praise for Angels

"I first visited Paul Lambillion in 2000. With his help, the spirit of Jane Austen contacted me. Together, with Jane and other angels, we were guided to so much significant information and many important revelations in our struggle to authenticate a portrait of my husband's "Aunt Jane." I heartily recommend this beautiful book to anyone who searches for knowledge of the angels, the afterlife, and for wise counselling prompted by faith and love and the quest for truth."

ANNE RICE, OWNER OF THE RICE PORTRAIT OF JANE AUSTEN

"Angels Looking Through, Stories of Contact With Remarkable Spirits, is an insightful and uplifting gift—a true gem, for those who value learning about the profound spiritual bond with life."

DIANE HAEGER, BESTSELLING AUTHOR

"Paul Lambillion shares hopeful and joyful stories of his encounters with departed souls in *Angels Looking Through.* There is just as much warmth as there is wisdom in his words, making the reading experience feel like a personal conversation with a gifted clairvoyant. The first half of the book will open your heart, while the second half will open your mind to fascinating possibilities about the afterlife."

CANDI SARY, AUTHOR OF AWARD WINNING NOVEL, BLACK CROW WHITE LIE

"From his recollections taken from the many and diverse sessions held with his clients, Paul presents proof of a continuing existence after physical death. His years of experience and expertise of the human aura, further endorse this. Not only will this book help those seeking confirmation that our departed loved ones continue their connection with us, but it is also a useful guide for those who wish to develop their mediumistic skills."

GRAHAM DAVIES, HEALER, COUNSELLOR, CLAIRVOYANT

"Beautiful. Straightforward and easy to read. Paul keeps everything very real on a subject that can easily be misinterpreted or sensationalised."

TAMMY MCLELLAN, PARENT & MASSAGE THERAPIST

"Paul Lambillion makes the extraordinary seem almost ordinary. In this book, the best news for me was that when we get to Heaven, we get to choose to either go on a vacation or to take up a great work, usually related to our interests and passions during our earthly lives. It is comforting to know that our loved ones watch over us and are there in our times of need."

DR. SOPHIA TWAROG, ECONOMIST

"Paul Lambillion writes with elegance from a down-to-earth perspective of heaven sent experiences. His work reveals a message of great power for all of humankind in times when we as a species need the utmost connection to real spirituality. His work inspires harmony within, an essential element in allowing each of us to bring peace to our beautiful planet."

DAVID M. BLAIR, MARRIAGE & FAMILY THERAPIST, LMFT

"A refreshing change from many of the books written on this subject. Paul's writing is easily accessible and humorous, weaving a story that appeals to all readers and especially those who seek a greater understanding and meaning to their lives."

MARGARET MITTINS-LADD, CHAIR OF THE INTERNATIONAL HEALING FELLOWSHIP

"Whether you believe or not, *Angels Looking Through* is a fascinating look at spiritual beings and how they interact with our world. Clearly, Lambillion has a perfect view of the unseen world around us and the talent to present it with credence and lucidity."

MIKE MILLER, AUTHOR

"Paul's effortless communications with Angels are truly loving and reassuring. We gain a better understanding of the next dimension and may even begin to feel more at ease about our own journey into the next world. At the same time, it is so very healing to realize that those who move on love, forgive, support and try to encourage us on our life paths. This is a unique and precious book that you will want to refer back to many times."

KATJA STRASSER, NUMEROLOGIST AND HEALER

"I was reassured, inspired and encouraged to be more confident in my own awareness of 'angels' and the messages they bring. The book flows in a way which carries the reader on a journey of discovery. Stories filled with hope, pain, laughter and the joy of renewed contact with loved ones who have passed over.

Paul has a knack of making the 'supernatural' seem natural. I also found this book educational, answering many of my own previously unanswered questions. I am sure that 'Angels Looking Through' will bring comfort to many looking for more evidence of life everlasting."

SHIRLEY BILLES, PERSONAL AND SPIRITUAL DEVELOPMENT CONSULTANT

ANGELS
Looking Through

Stories of Contact with Remarkable Spirits

ANGELS
Looking
Through

Stories of Contact with Remarkable Spirits

PAUL LAMBILLION

TOP READS PUBLISHING, INC

Vista, California

First Edition

ISBN-10: 0-9964860-3-8
ISBN-13: 978-0-9964860-3-3

Library of Congress Control Number: 2016954113

Angels Looking Through: Stories of Contact with Remarkable Spirits is published by: Top Reads Publishing, Inc., 1035 E. Vista Way, Suite 205, Vista, CA, 92084-4213 USA

For information please direct emails to: topreadspublishing@gmail.com or visit our website: www.TopReadsPublishing.com

Editing: Deborah Smith Parker, Jean Ardell
Cover design: Teri Rider
Book layout and typography: Teri Rider & Associates

Printed in the United States of America

Dedication

This book is dedicated to all those marvellous souls and wonderful people, both in this world and beyond, who have helped me, supported me, encouraged me and so enriched my own life.

Thank you so much. I love you.

Contents

Introduction

We were sitting having supper together as we had done so many times. My old friend sparkled with energy, full of her usual inquisitiveness and humour. Our conversation was as lively as it had ever been. Two weeks later she was gone. She died suddenly at her home. All that was left for me, her many other friends and her family were a few possessions and the dear memories of her times with us. No more jokes to share, no more of her gentle scolding of my sometimes silly thoughts, no more anything.

It happens every day. Somewhere an aware, intelligent, breathing, smiling, or frowning individual who has shared some part of their life with us just stops being. They leave, and for many of us, after a few hymns, prayers, and eulogies, it is over. Life for them has ended and we are left feeling diminished, having lost something uniquely precious.

We miss their energy, their idiosyncrasies, their laughter, even their grumpy moments, and most of all, their love. Oh how we would love to enjoy just one more cup of tea with them, listen to their awful jokes again, and hold their hand when we are low.

It is inconceivable that something as remarkable as a living, walking, talking human being can completely disappear from our lives never to be seen or heard again. Even science, in its matter-of-fact way tells us that nothing ever really dies but simply changes state as it flows through our eternal cosmos. Energy moves on into another space, as do the particles that it once embraced and vivified. So what happens to what once was you and me? Do we just evaporate like an early morning mist in the rising sun's warmth?

Ever since I was a boy I have seen the "dead," those no longer in a physical body but existing in a world parallel to this planet. For me they are still alive, thinking, fully functioning and apparently freed from the trials and tribulations we who are left behind continue to wade through day by day. What we call death is no such thing. Our essence, that which we revealed through our human lives, continues on another journey, somewhere else but still able to interact with us here.

This book is about my path of discovery. It is a book of stories, and, where possible, explanations of unusual events that have punctuated much of my life. It concerns some of the conversations I have had with those who have died but live on elsewhere, seeking to contact us and reassure us that death is not what we think it is. I hope it will answer some readers' questions, comfort some, and provoke others, challenging the belief that this life is all there is, or offering hope to those who doubt but wish it to be true; that mum, dad, auntie and other beloveds haven't disappeared into nothingness but continue on as we will also do one day. No longer a brief life lived in vain to no long-term purpose but a chapter in a never-ending tale.

The beings I have encountered are true angels, ones who look through at us from their new existence, seeking to bring us a message; one that says there is no finality in death, but rather we move on to fresh experience and purpose, existing in a new state. Birth and death are no more than entrances and exits to and from a particular stage we call this physical planet earth.

These angels are here with us for those who have ears to hear, eyes to see, and hearts to feel their presence close to us.

I invite you to read, with open heart and mind, the stories selected from over thirty years of consultations as a medium and healer. Consider what their message is for you. Whatever it proves to be, I hope it brings something precious to you.

CHAPTER 1

He Must be a Fraud

A couple came to see me. As is usually the case before a first meeting, I knew nothing about them. Tom, the husband, took the first appointment, while his wife, Megan, waited outside. Tom was a well-dressed man with a quiet presence. He didn't seem particularly interested in communication from beings in other worlds but was more concerned that I help him with his career by analyzing his brightly coloured aura. A study of this electro-magnetic phenomenon, radiating from all living beings and physical objects, can be very useful when seeking to give guidance and direction. Over the past thirty years I have done this type of work for many, including corporate clients. (I'll address this topic more thoroughly in Chapter 12.)

By clairvoyantly observing the colours, frequencies, and images in the aura that radiated from Tom, I could see he had been a success in popular music. As the session proceeded he spoke of his many hit records and a few film themes he had written, especially in the USA. He now had reached a crossroads in his career. He was seeking direction for a record deal with some new material. When Tom's session ended he left the room and his wife's session began. I know he found the session useful as he often returned.

Bright eyed and articulate, Megan sat opposite to me, appearing a little nervous as folk often do when first consulting a psychic or clairvoyant. I'm not sure what they expect—something rather theatrical maybe, or a dimly lit room with an eccentric medium, eyes rolling, uttering forth in strange tongues. I suspect my rather ordinary appearance, seated in a comfortable lounge overlooking the Kent countryside, may have disappointed her a little.

As I looked at her, one or two images came to me. I described them as clearly as possible. They were from situations in her life and promptings from angels and unseen visitors seeking to make contact with her. These are the first snippets of information, as the link is made with both the visiting angel and the client—a birthday date maybe, the unusually painted door of a house the angel lived in, the special brooch or ring they wore and left behind, and so on. On this occasion, in the early moments of the consultation, the information I shared with Megan was not always especially clear, but this happens sometimes. It was a little random and fragmented as one may experience on a poor telephone line.

"I don't understand any of that," she replied, politely but firmly shaking her head.

I continued to describe other scenes that came into my view. They meant nothing to her. It is not unusual for a client's apprehensions to block the psychic link between them and the clairvoyant, especially in the early part of a session when the connection is still being established. This can be for several reasons: the client may not understand the message being relayed at that moment, or could have simply forgotten the events or circumstances being communicated but may acknowledge them later; or the message contains information the client does not yet know; or, very common on a first visit to a clairvoyant, they simply feel nervous. The psychic knows the images and information are correct, but also that they are just not being recognised at that moment.

As the session progressed, Megan's rejection of what I told her increased to the point where I began to wonder if I was in the right profession. My attempts to inject a little humour into the situation bore some fruit when Megan began to smile a little more, looking more relaxed. Then, what I hoped was the moment to rescue the situation occurred. A woman from the other world (often called the spirit world by many mediums) who had been attempting to communicate, walked through the room and stood beside Megan. The lady smiled sweetly, pointing at the necklace Megan was wearing, made from small beads of amber.

"There is an elegant, refined lady trying to communicate with us." I said. "She was well-educated, she says, and she is showing me that she was skilled in embroidery and needlepoint." Our angel visitor was demonstrating to me her proficiency in needlework, holding a needle and thread in one hand and a stretched embroidery cloth in the other.

"I can see that she always pinned her hair up neatly and wore unfussy, smart dresses. She looks like a teacher and she's telling me she was the owner of the necklace you are wearing."

Megan looked surprised. "I don't recognise the woman you are describing. And this necklace was owned by my husband Tom's grandmother. She was not refined at all, I understand."

The angel communicator looked as frustrated as I felt. However, I was determined to press on so I continued to describe the scene unfolding before me.

"She always wore smart gloves. Never felt properly dressed without them," I told Megan.

The lady continued to show various things to me—the large house she stayed in with a spacious entrance hall and grand winding staircase. I could see the children she was connected to in this grand building and the wonderful paintings and glass display cabinets containing fine china.

"No, I'm sorry; I can't understand any of this," my client protested.

In one final foray, I was shown the grounds of the building. A large driveway and beautiful gardens—gardens I had seen earlier in the meeting. Megan continued to shake her head, by now looking a little embarrassed at my apparent failure to come up with anything vaguely recognisable.

Our angel visitor appeared to be even more frustrated. So was I. However, she again pointed to the necklace and then at herself, smiling as she did so.

"She insists that was her necklace," I told Megan.

Megan again shook her head, uttering a polite "no" as she rose to leave the room. She thanked me for my time and efforts, clearly disappointed with the experience. At that point I had no idea if I would ever see either of them again. Although I, too, was dissatisfied, I continued with my next appointments. Megan and Tom related the rest of the story to me much later after we became friends. They decided to enlighten me with their subsequent discoveries after their first session. They told me they had discussed their experience as they drove home. Tom was pleased with the advice I had given to him, but Megan was not impressed. They came to the conclusion that I was probably a fraud who had hit lucky with Tom, making fortuitous guesses that happened to fit, but that generally I was either attempting to make a fast buck from the gullible and vulnerable or that I was simply delusional.

Tom told me that sometime later when they had tea with his mother, Megan wore the amber necklace she had been wearing when she came to see me. The time they spent with me came up in the conversation. Megan was still wrestling with the discrepancy between the elegant lady I had described and the rough and ready, unrefined woman who had been Tom's grandmother. Seeking merely to confirm what she believed to be true, she asked her mother-in-law to verify that the necklace she had been given had indeed, originally belonged to Tom's grandmother.

They were both stunned when Tom's mother told them the necklace had belonged to Tom's Great Aunt Violet, not his grandmother at all. Megan quickly asked to know more about Aunt Violet.

The description and information that Tom's mother gave surprised them even more.

Aunt Violet had indeed been a woman of culture, quite proper, who always acted appropriately. She had worked as a governess to young children in a grand country house. The house, which Tom's mother had visited, had a large staircase rising from the entrance hall, with fine paintings hung on the walls she recalled. Tom said to me, "You should have seen the look on Meg's face!"

Tom was also affected by this news. "I felt the hairs stand up on the back of my neck when I heard this," he confessed.

His mother continued her account, telling them how Aunt Violet loved the gardens of the house and in her spare time would often sit outside doing needlework—she was a very accomplished embroiderer. Megan was by now apparently completely taken aback.

"Did she wear gloves?" she wanted to know.

Aunt Violet, she was told, never went out without her gloves, considering a lady wasn't properly dressed without them. When taking tea she drank only from a bone china cup;

she was particular about that too. And the house had large display cabinets in the hallway that were filled with expensive china and pottery. Tom's mother thought the owner had been a collector of antique porcelain.

I understand Tom and Megan drove home in silence that day. Needless to say, Tom and especially Megan, changed their view of the time we first spent together, and I am grateful for their story. They certainly no longer considered me to be a fraud.

I am also grateful for the visit and persistence of Tom and Megan's angel, Great Aunt Violet, who took the time to visit us from another world, revealing that life in some way continues after physical death, and that angels come to tell us so.

Does it sometimes fail?

Not all sessions with clients appear to be successes.

An elderly man sat with me, arms folded, his face lined with a slight frown. He barely spoke as I gave my usual preamble to put him at ease and explain what I would try to do before looking clairvoyantly to see which angel visitors were around him.

I described the first angel to him.

"No. Don't know who that is," he responded. Then silence.

I continued with little success so I went on to describe another of his spiritual friends, who I could see had appeared and was standing close to him.

"Don't know him either," he replied again, rather gruffly. He was obviously unimpressed with my efforts. When describing the scene of a farm and its animals, which was being presented to me by a persistent angel, the old man's response was an equally sharp put down.

"You'd expect a farmer to have a farm wouldn't you?" he replied.

Up to that point I had no idea that he was a farmer but the fact that I was describing in detail the farm he had lived on since he was a boy, which was confirmed to me by his wife, did not satisfy him at all. He was clearly very sceptical about the whole process. It was an exhausting session for me, peppered with mostly negative reactions to all I said to him. I felt as droopy as the wild moustache that hung down from his top lip.

In the story I just related one could see it's possible for clients not to understand or recognise some and even all of what the medium is telling them. Mediums who are well trained and experienced will know that the information they perceive is real and related to the client, but somehow, it simply isn't registering with them, at least in that moment. Occasionally you may be fortunate, as I was with Tom and Megan, to discover that the things not initially accepted by the client are identified and verified later.

Both the client and the medium may at the time, view such difficult sessions as failures. All psychics and mediums will have such experiences, though mercifully few of them. On the other hand, I have received letters and emails, sometimes many years after the consultation, saying such things as "the appointment with you changed my life," or "everything you said proved to be true."

In a churlish mode I am inclined to mutter, "I wish you had told me sooner!"

So what happens in a session with a clairvoyant? What are the simple dynamics involved and why is it sometimes a success and, at other times, it seems to be less so?

What happens when Angels look through?
Seeing, hearing and feeling

All clairvoyants, mediums or psychics utilise certain psychic faculties when working with someone to look at their aura and energy system, or communicate the messages of angel visitors. These abilities exist in all of us, they are just more active and developed in a good medium who has learned how to manage and control them.

The first of these is clairvoyance itself, often used as a generic term to describe a psychic. It means, "clear seeing."

This is where I see the angel communicator and the things they wish to reveal to me, hoping that the client will recognise them by my description and know who the angel is. It's the means by which they seek to show themselves and try to prove their identity. The quality of these visions can vary from session to session, from day to day. Mediums are people, after all, and have good days and not so good days where personal stress, illness, or fatigue can inhibit the effectiveness of their psychic process.

With clairvoyance, sometimes the entire angel is clearly visible. Sometimes only a part of the angel can be seen, such as its face, or maybe just its silhouette. In most cases the angel will also show to the medium items or situations to help identify who they are—an unusually decorated wedding ring, the house they lived in with its door number, or maybe a favourite book they read many times, or the work they did.

Clairaudience or "clear hearing" occurs when the medium hears some or all that the angel wishes to say. This facility can also vary in quality from a distinct voice difficult to differentiate from an earthly human one, to an internal whispering echo resonating quietly in the skull. This is most useful for hearing the name the angel may wish to give.

The third means of communication is clairsentience or "clear feeling," in which mediums feel or sense information—they feel what is being said or shown to them. This faculty is especially active early on in a session where the medium is mentally attuning to and exploring the psychic energy around them. This enables them to sense and know when they are psychically connected to their client before their seeing or hearing takes over, although some clairvoyants rely mainly on clairsentience in most of their work. They feel what other psychics see. One dear old medium friend of mine works mainly through her clairsentience and she imparts wonderfully accurate angel information.

Most mediums and psychics use a combination of all three processes, with perhaps a predominating strength in one of them. I am predominantly clairvoyant, with some clairaudience, depending on the situation. Sometimes in a session the communication is mostly through my clairvoyant vision: in others my hearing of words and voices becomes more evident, complementing what I see. Some level of clairsentience is active in all my work as it is with all psychics.

While the blend of these abilities can vary from session to session and client to client, the nature of these faculties is difficult to explain further in simple terms but is perhaps best referred to in terms of frequencies.

We know that our world and, indeed, our universe is an amazing field of many different waves and frequencies—nothing is really solid. All we see and experience is a pulsing, moving sea of various vibrations in particle and waveforms. That is also true of our angel visitors and us.

The medium working with the more subtle of these forces around them has to attune to a whole range of individuals and frequencies in their work and will therefore initiate, usually subconsciously, whatever mix of clairvoyance, clairaudience and clairsentience is appropriate for the individual they are dealing with. Sometimes it is easier than on other occasions to do this and accounts for the occasional "failure" or "difficult" encounter when there is literally a frequency incompatibility between the medium and the client. This can be because the client is nervous about what the medium may say, especially if it is his or her first experience. Or they may be distressed over bereavement or some other difficulty, though I find the psychic barrier these situations create is usually quickly dissolved.

The sceptic

When consulting a medium or psychic, especially during a first-time visit, a degree of healthy scepticism is useful, accompanied by open mindedness and a willingness to experience the possibility that something special may be taking place.

I have seen many sceptics won over by a good evidential clairvoyant experience, often changing their view of life and its meaning forever, especially when an angel loved one makes very clear contact with them. Often, the presence and rising frequency of a well-attuned medium's aura touches the client enabling him or her to also feel the presence of an angel for the first time. A client's tears of joy often follow this experience.

Some individuals however, seem to want to do all they can to debunk the whole process and the healing it may bring.

I have experienced downright hostility. Mediums are highly sensitive people and a client who wishes them to fail, sending out their own destructive waves of negative thought may well appear to succeed sometimes. On the very rare occasions where this had been especially clear to me and the client is seeking to play mental games, I have stopped a consultation—I have no wish to try to prove anything to anyone who has such a firmly closed or even aggressive mind. As the author Roald Dahl wrote, "Those who never look for magic will never find it."

Whatever the situation, and even if the descriptions given are occasionally poor, good mediums know what they are offering is correct despite any rejection by the client. A good medium's work is generated by love and a desire for truth, and not for battles of the ego. They will generally not be deterred by foolish, destructive antics.

The clergyman

While on holiday in the Canary Islands some years ago, I was asked by a client who lived there to take a day so I could offer some appointments.

I agreed. My last session of the day was with an older, sweet-natured man. His main angel contact was a young man who had been his son. The angel described to me how he had been killed in a road accident in England whilst on his way home from work. He had previously phoned his father with whom he was living at the time, to say he would be back later than usual.

The angel informed me that a wheel from a fast moving lorry severed from its axle, bounced along the carriageway in front of his car, smashed through his windscreen, and killed him instantly. His father was moved to tears by his words, but eventually was comforted by the news that his son still existed and was fine in his new world. Afterwards, over a cup of tea,

I discovered my client was a clergyman, spending the last years of his ministry working on the islands as a chaplain to the Anglican community. He was indeed a lovely man and our meeting had been of enormous help and comfort to him.

A little while later when he had returned to the U.K., the chaplain called and asked if he could bring two friends, a husband and wife, to see me.

When we met it was obvious the woman viewed me with more than a little suspicion. During her session I remember feeling her resistance. Whilst I cannot recall the details of what took place, I do remember feeling that I had done quite well despite the hostility I sensed dominating the appointment. She was polite to me but rather cold, clearly having very serious doubts about the whole idea of meeting me at all, let alone receiving a message or two from an unseen visitor.

When we had finished, they all left and I thought no more about it except that it was good to see John the chaplain again. He was one of those rare people that simply radiate goodness.

Then, a week or so later I received a letter from the woman John had brought to see me.

She wrote that she was worried about John when he told her of his session with me. A devout Christian, she was doubtful about such things as clairvoyance, mediums, and the like. She thought I may have been a con man who had misled her dear grieving friend, and she had come to see me in order to prove herself correct and expose me. This explained the difficulty I had experienced in the meeting, and how the communications I had succeeded in establishing were only moderately successful.

The letter continued by saying that she had changed her mind. Whatever it was I did, it was genuine and helpful and also challenging to her existing beliefs. She also commented that I was a nice caring man. Praise indeed from a sceptic who looked now to be at least open to the idea that angels indeed may look through to contact us.

Such events teach the medium much about themselves and what they do, especially the patience and resilience needed in such work, not to mention stamina.

As a wonderful medium once told me, "My dear Paul, if you do five readings in a day, one will be excellent and will go well, one will be difficult and you will feel like you are climbing a high greasy wall, and the other three will be somewhere in between these two."

That seems about right to me.

CHAPTER 2

Trusting Angel Voices: The Importance of Discernment

⁓≈⁓

*M*any of us hear voices that we know are not of this world. Sometimes they are inner ones, our own thoughts and dialogue echoing in our heads. Sometimes they seem to be from outside, separate from us, coming from another source, perhaps as a loud whisper. It is especially common after a loved one has passed on, for those close to them to report hearing or seeing them, certainly for a while at least. The emotional intensity and powerful feelings triggered in us by such grief may briefly heighten our awareness and sensitivity.

It is not always easy to discern whether it is some kind of delusion or something much more meaningful, an actual communication from one of our angels wanting us to know they are all right and still exist. But, with experience and practice, it is possible to discern if it is a loved one because the message they give will be a simple "I'm okay" or "I love you still," accompanied by a few poignant memories to help us recognize who it is. These angel messengers will not try to tell us what to do or run our lives for us, but they may point out some serious avoidable danger of which we are unaware.

Not all invisible voices are reliable. Some are, whilst others are less so, requiring us to be cautious and to learn to understand the difference. I will discuss this more fully in later chapters of this book. I have seen sad things occur as a consequence of following the advice of a voice, initially seeming reliable but then becoming misleading at a crucial moment. Such voices tell us what we want to hear, even flattering us somewhat.

A cautionary tale

About twenty-five years ago I met a man who, in early middle age, discovered he had mediumistic and psychic abilities. He was intelligent, smartly dressed, and communicated well. He had started to give readings and to address public meetings. A new world was opening for him and he was very keen to embrace it and give his life to the work of comforting and helping others with his gift, a noble sentiment.

At a public meeting, where I was acting as chairman, he had been invited to demonstrate his gifts. It was a reasonably successful evening, with many who attended appreciating what he had done. His abilities were a little raw, needing refinement, but he certainly made connections at times with some genuine visiting angels who were known to members of the audience, bringing their wonderful yet simple messages of love and remembrance.

Afterwards, he came up to me smiling broadly, obviously pleased with what he had done.

"Do you know, spirits told me I would be on the radio and I was. Then they said I would be on television, and I was. Next they said I would write a book, which I have, and I will try to get it published as they said I will be successful in doing so." He paused for a while, then went on. "They have told me to give up my job and work full time as a psychic medium. I have handed in my notice and will become self-employed as the spirit voices told me to, so I can do this work full time from now on."

I felt anxiety as he spoke but didn't wish to dampen his enthusiasm for the new life he envisaged and that the voices, proving reliable thus far, had encouraged him to follow so radically. Besides, a golden rule for all psychics is never offering unsolicited advice. My feelings were further compounded when his rather less voluble wife informed me that she was also giving up her job to help him in his work. Apparently the voices had also suggested this. They had been right so far, so it seemed logical to take their advice again. But I was uneasy about it all.

Sadly, the whole venture ended in disaster, as I feared. This couple ended up in severe financial difficulty. He eventually had to seek his old job back at a lower pay grade to start paying off the debt they had accumulated. The promised book was never published. So two nice although misguided people became totally disillusioned with all matters spiritual, and especially the guidance of voices.

Learning about voices

It took years for me to learn how I could discriminate between good angel voices and other less sophisticated promptings—not an easy skill to acquire. The church has wrestled with this issue since the early Christian era, the case of Joan of Arc being one notable example. Church dignitaries found it difficult to discern whether her voices were from God and his Angels as she claimed they were, or from demons. Personally, I would be extremely suspicious and dismissive of any voice that encouraged me to harm or hurt people. Despite subsequent rosy massaging of her tale by history, she wasn't always well guided as her less lauded, failed military exploits and ultimate demise suggest. Being burned at the stake may have been common in mediaeval Europe, but it was certainly not God's idea.

My voices are usually accompanied by the visual appearance of the angel communicator. In fact I see them much more than I hear them. Sound, trustworthy angel messages are always couched in love, are gentle and caring, supporting our best choices but never dictating to us on serious issues. They know we have to make our own decisions, so they won't interfere in our sacred freedoms.

There are some basic rules I have learned concerning voices that come from our angel loved ones in the higher world:

🕊 Never suspend your own common-sense judgement and say, "A voice said to do this or do that." The voice may be right, but unless you have developed a good method of knowing which voices you can trust and which you cannot, it is best to wait and see, learning from a good, experienced medium or psychic over a period of years.

🕊 A true angel voice will never interfere with your free will, your own choices, especially important ones.

🕊 Angel voices you can trust will never tell you to do something that would expose you to unnecessary risk, harm you, or encourage actions that would hurt you or another. And sadly, to the uneducated psychic ear, it is not uncommon for a questionable voice to predict and then seem to provide a few treats, including finding the odd car parking space for you, or predicting a new job, before letting you down or advising you badly, as I just described.

An early lesson: "Don't tell him"

As a boy I heard many voices and saw many apparitions and angel visitors who, I quickly realised, were apparent only to me. Most I didn't know or recognise so I ignored them. I recall one particular day, however—I was about five years old at the time—when I should have heeded the voice's advice. But I had not reached the stage of awareness necessary to discriminate effectively between the different types. It is an example of the bewilderment a particularly psychic child or adult may experience when their abilities are raw and undeveloped.

My father liked to place small bets on the horses at the weekend. It was always small amounts of money, a shilling here and a shilling there, something many working class men and women did then, which he persisted with all his life. He wasn't a real gambler but just liked a "flutter" now and again. I remember him scrutinising carefully the racing pages at the back of the newspaper, marking with his pen the one or two horses he fancied might win a race. Sometimes he won and sometimes he lost, but it was just a bit of weekend fun for him in an otherwise hard life. It was not long after the war and things were still tough. My mother wasn't particularly keen on this activity of his, perhaps thinking the pennies gambled should have been added to our meager food budget.

On this particular day, Dad was seated at the kitchen table with the horse racing pages opened in front of him and, as I often did, I peered round his shoulder. Next to one of the names on the page he was looking at I could see a small bright light. I knew the horse whose name was next to the light would win its race and I was about to tell him when a gentle voice said, "Better not tell him, Paul!" It was a real voice but I could see no one else in the room as I looked around. I could not only hear this voice, I could feel it too, deep in my body, something I learned later is another of several indicators of a true angel voice I can trust when communicating with me.

"Don't tell him," it came again.

However, I ignored the voice and blurted out to my dad that I knew this particular horse would win the race. I remember its name to this day. It was called "Arabian Nights." Why I finally did it I don't know; perhaps a little boy wishing to impress his father.

Dad turned and smiled, saying he doubted it would as it was an "outsider," but he would put a very small bet on it for me. I was thrilled and, true to form, I received a few pennies a day later as my horse galloped home a triumphant winner! Dad, very fond of me anyway, now thought I was a star. In the coming weeks I was able to continue to do the same for him—but secretly, as he had instructed me not tell my mother or sister, and I obeyed.

Somehow Mum found out about our little arrangement and was not at all happy. Whilst she was a lady who liked the mysterious, and as a consequence of her Irish background was incredibly superstitious, she saw such things as a boy who could predict the "winners" as next to the diabolical, and she made her feelings known in no uncertain terms. It was not a happy moment! I really should have heeded this voice but at that point I had no way of knowing its authenticity. So, as the golden rule concerning actions and giving advice suggests—"If in doubt, don't."

Learning and listening

There were many things I needed to learn on my pathway to healing and mediumistic work.

Most important was meditation. This fundamental

spiritual discipline must be mastered before all else, enabling the individual to be well grounded while simultaneously unfolding a deepening inner connection with his or her spiritual nature. If you are going to communicate with the spirits of others you must get to know your own a little better first. I studied pranayama breathing techniques, learned from a swami I got chatting with in a library one day. Effective management of the breath brings greater control of one's energies and forces, vital in all psycho-spiritual work, in fact, vital no matter what work we do. In my opinion, until we have learned something of the art of breathing we shouldn't go any further in psychic and mediumistic unfoldment. As our psychic mechanism awakens we become more sensitive to the many subtle forces around us, especially atmospheres. For a time, this can be a difficult experience for some as the necessary adjustments take place within them. Good breath management strengthens both our energy bodies and nervous systems, essential for those who seek to function effectively as a medium, a healer, or as any kind of practitioner working intimately with others.

I studied many forms of meditative practice and philosophy—Buddhist, Huna, Transcendental Meditation (T.M.), and anything else I could find. I went to lectures, took private classes and read avidly, gradually distilling from this ocean of ideas a basic philosophy of my own. During this period my intuition, or inner teacher, developed wonderfully endowing me with a strong sense of what was right and good for me as an individual to pursue, as well as what wasn't. It was imperative that I become more in control of myself first.

Eventually, I attended meetings where mediums were demonstrating or lecturing, learning as much as I could. I briefly visited a "development" group organised by a medium but didn't find it useful as the quality of teaching was poor. It seemed to me that many psychics and mediums lacked an understanding of how they facilitated their craft, regardless of how good they were. From a teaching perspective such a lack of knowledge is rather limiting. It was fortunate that I had been a natural clairvoyant since childhood and I was learning on my own how to manage my abilities rather than unlock them from scratch as some others were doing. Often, good teachers appeared as I was ready for them, and for the sincere spiritual student I find this always happens.

Much of my learning was informal, more a matter of my humble curiosity leading me as I attended spiritualist meetings and rubbed shoulders with some excellent (and also not so excellent) mediums. I watched, I listened, and I learned. I sought their advice, guidance, and assessment of my abilities, my strengths, and my weaknesses. I was encouraged by them to observe what was good practice and what was not.

Some, generally older than I was at the time, became friends and invited me to work with them. A good experienced medium will know if you are ready and right for such an opportunity. The budding medium learns through a process of osmosis as much as through direct instruction, when spending time with those already gifted and experienced. I was able to do this and it became the main aspect of my psychic education.

On the advice of one famous medium I respected, I formed my own development group with some friends who, unselfishly and spontaneously, volunteered to help me—I didn't have to ask them when they heard what I was considering. This enabled me to practice regularly each week for seven years, developing a growing awareness of different levels of consciousness. I learned how to go into deep trance states using my breathing skills.

Gradually my psychic abilities became more secure and more reliable, as did my discernment of voices. That "knowingness" necessary in all good psychics flowered in me. My work as a healer also grew. However, I saw and still see myself as the eternal student, learning and improving wherever I can. It takes patience, practice, discipline, modesty, sincerity, a sense of humour (particularly important for me), and the ability to deal with disappointment.

In my view it is also important to study not just mediumship but all aspects and traditions of the spiritual life. We should seek to be a balanced, awakening individual whatever we wish to do and be in life. And resist becoming a recluse. While there is need for some quiet at times, we strengthen best by exploring life and living it to the full. It was Dr. Carl Jung who said that no one could individuate on top of a mountain.

In this regard I took up martial arts to toughen my mind and body relationship, practised prayer and self-development processes, especially forgiveness. I visited art galleries regularly and attended concerts—everything from Monteverdi Vespers to The Rolling Stones. My creativity was nourished by writing and drawing.

All the truly great mediums I have been privileged to know have loved life, enjoyed being with others, and were spiritually inquisitive, but also needed occasional quiet moments. Being a rounded human being equips us better for whatever we seek to do. So I became more curious than ever about life in all its aspects, not purely the psychic.

As I unfolded my knowledge, I learned how to discriminate between good and less trustworthy voices, between the light of a true angel and other phenomena such as thought forms and ghosts, which I will discuss more in later chapters.

"Tell her it's me"—bending the rules a little

One of the benefits of carefully learning and abiding by the proper protocols is, strange as it may seem, that it enables one to have confidence in evaluating situations in which a little bending of the rules may be permissible, as the following experience illustrates. I mean "bend" and not "break."

As I mentioned earlier, an essential rule for any psychic or medium is never to give information, especially advice, to people you are with, no matter how much the communicating visitor might press us to do so. The exception would be if the person is consulting you professionally or a very good friend who you are sure may be interested. Even then, be cautious. Quite apart from professional protocols such as confidentiality, appropriateness and so on, it may actually frighten, even offend some if they find you are talking to their "dead" loved ones. And it may result in you being treated like a party entertainer, something to be avoided at all costs in my opinion, although it can be difficult to resist.

In the early 1990s, whilst working in Germany, I experienced a really compelling angel voice.

I had been dining with a few friends, and the convivial evening was drawing to a close, one or two people having already left. Seated next to me was a woman who had translated the seminar I'd presented earlier that day. Joan was an American doctor who had lived and worked in Germany for a number of years, and was especially interested in spiritual matters. She was an excellent help for someone like me whose grasp of

German language was limited—I could order a beer, but that was about it.

Our conversation had progressed to cover sport, politics, the merits of a decent bottle of wine and many other general topics when a voice began to talk to me. I could feel at once that it was a genuine angel loved one trying to contact Joan.

"It's me. Please tell her. Tell her it's me."

I had learned to talk back mentally to such voices, by now able to discern the trustworthy ones. Its owner had clearly been waiting his chance, using significant energy to break through my psychic "switched off" mode (which, whilst still penetrable a little, is usually firmly in place, filtering things out on most social occasions or life would become intolerable). Whoever he was, the love he felt for Joan was quite palpable, strong and warm.

"Please be still," I requested of the voice.

But he was unperturbed, what you might call a rather persistent angel.

"I loved her apple pie," he went on. "She'd cook the apples from the trees in our garden," the voice continued. By this time I was aware of a man, appearing to be in his late 60s, smiling at me under a baseball cap. It had a name printed on it, which I could hardly recognise, but it looked like Joe or Joey. "Please tell her I love her. And that she will be happy if she decides to go back."

At that moment, Joan looked at me wistfully, as if she sensed what was going on. The tone of her voice had changed, becoming heavier, less lively. The others still seated at the table were busy speaking amongst themselves in German, inattentive to our conversation.

"Paul." I remember the sigh as she spoke my name. "I am mulling over something right now. I realise you are off duty, so to speak...." Her words faded away, suggesting slight embarrassment at what she was preparing to ask me.

"Look, Joan." I decided to follow the voice. "Are you thinking of going back?" Back to where I didn't know, though I assumed it was to the States. A big, big smile opened out across her face.

"Yes I am. To New Jersey." She was delighted I had asked the question. "Tell me more, Paul. Please."

"Well someone's here, wearing a blue baseball cap, says you will be happy if you go back. And he liked the apple pies you made; from the garden were they... those apples?" I asked.

Her smile broadened; her eyes misted with tears. "Say hi to Dad. Tell him I love him. So does Mom. He still wearing that old hat? He had it on the day he died."

It was indeed the angel voice of her father, Joe, who had died two years previously. Joan's long-term relationship to a physician in Germany had broken up painfully, and she saw no reason to remain there any longer. She had been investigating job possibilities and vacancies in New Jersey, where her mom lived and where I believe those much remembered apple trees were. She had more or less decided to go home to the United States soon, and wanted to run the idea past me. Her angel Dad's words just helped her to trust her own judgement.

"Tell him thank you. Thanks, Dad. I love you."

"He loves you too," I replied.

I love you. The three best words any voice can ever, ever say.

I am so glad I listened to Joe's voice. So was Joan.

Following are many stories of such voices and appearances from beloved and interesting angels, reminding us that death isn't what we think it is. Not at all.

CHAPTER 3

Hauntings

~~~

*W*e all seem to be stirred by rumours of what is commonly called a "ghost." Most of us like stories of the unknown, the unexplainable, especially when recounted on a dark winter's night, in a room illuminated only by the flickering light of a candle. Such tales set our hearts racing. There is something in us that loves to be both frightened and thrilled. The truth of this is evident when we reflect on the popularity of stories of spirits, ghosts, ghouls and vampires that proliferate in movies, books, and on television programmes created to satisfy this strange human need.

However, both adults and children can be adversely affected by this barrage of occult material now available at the press of a button. Sometimes anxious parents bring their terrified children to see me, unable to sleep because their naturally sensitive imaginations have been over-stimulated by a horror movie, seen without supervision on a friend's DVD player. Frightened adults, who are convinced they have an evil presence in their home like the one they saw on TV, also arrive at my door.

It's one thing to watch a film or read a book that provides vicarious thrills. It is quite another to have a personal, "face to face" encounter with something or someone reaching out to us from the invisible worlds beyond this material life.

A Call for help from the police

As my reputation as a healer and clairvoyant grew, local agencies such as the police and Citizens Advice Bureau (which in the United Kingdom gives free, wide ranging advice to those who need it and don't know where to find it) began to direct people to me when they had a problem, usually described as a "haunting" or "spooky goings on."

I remember the first call I ever received from a police station, asking me for my help.

"Mr Lambillion?"

"Yes."

The policeman introduced himself, continuing in an uncertain voice, "Sir, we have some people here who are having a strange problem, and we believe it is your sort of thing. Would you mind if we pass your telephone number on to them, so they might contact you?"

"That's quite okay, officer," I replied, trying to assuage his obvious embarrassment in having to be involved in what he obviously considered a peculiar request. I told him to give them my phone number and tell them to contact me to make an appointment. I had already seen several police officers as private clients, so I assumed my name was known through my contact with them.

In this instance, "my sort of thing" proved to be three very anxious young women who had experienced some remarkable phenomena while driving along a local stretch of the A-11 trunk road near the village of Elveden, in England. Her two friends who were with her when the events occurred corroborated the story. Even though they were agitated on the night they visited my house, they didn't seem to be the usual thrill-seeker types. I found them to be articulate and generally well-grounded ladies.

Mrs Macdonald, the driver, sat on my settee between her two friends and told her story. She was composed but a little nervous. A few years earlier, John, an American airman stationed on the local Lakenheath Base with her husband, had been killed in an accident at a notorious accident "black spot" on this stretch of the A-11 trunk road. John had been a dear friend to both her and her husband and his sudden death was quite a shock to them. Recently, when travelling along this same road, she began to experience several unusual and frightening phenomena.

"As I approached the place where John was killed," she said, "the car became unbearably cold—freezing cold."

"Yes, that's right—freezing," her friends echoed.

"The temperature went down and down and down until we were all shivering," one of her companions added.

Mrs Macdonald went on to describe the cool mist that had descended upon the car. "Even the windows misted up," she said, the level of her alarm palpably rising. "Then it went mad. The steering wheel would go out of control, like it had a mind of its own. I'd be aware of John, almost like hearing his voice. And then ..." I remember her swallowing hard as she tried to continue, "... then the lights went funny, flashing on and off, up and down at random. I was doing nothing to make this happen."

Mrs Macdonald was quite animated now, her eyes wide open, moistened by small tears.

"Cars stopped to see what was happening. No one would come close. Even the police were nervous when they turned up. They couldn't work it out either and told me to get the car checked."

"They were wetting themselves, weren't they?" she asked her two friends, who nodded in confirmation. I could see they were beginning to feel a little relieved that I didn't react as if they were mad and saw that I may be able to help them.

"You believe us, don't you?"

I remember smiling, and reassuring them that I was sure we could sort it out. I enquired whether any of them had been tinkering with psychic phenomena, such as trying to read tarot cards, playing with an Ouija board, or pendulum since these kinds of experimentation are often precursors to such events. Untutored psychic dabbling is unwise and may open a door on experiences of an occult nature that can be difficult for the uninitiated to control and understand.

They assured me they had not, although Mrs Macdonald had recently given birth and was suffering from mild postnatal depression. This caught my attention since emotional disruption often precipitates unusual experiences of a psycho-spiritual nature, which then, unfortunately, are dismissed as some temporary psychosis or as delusion.

I decided it was best to experience this myself. Whenever possible, I try to visit the scene, as well as question the individuals involved to ensure they are genuine, even if their imagination may be on overdrive at the time. Mrs Macdonald told me that a subsequent check at the garage detected no discernible faults with the car, neither in the steering nor the electrical system.

I found all three ladies consistent in their stories. So, off we went to drive along the A-11 to the place at the centre of the story. I sat in the front of the car with Mrs Macdonald and her two friends sat in the back. I also invited two friends to follow us in their car, primarily as witnesses, but also as backup in case there were actual mechanical problems with the car.

The journey went smoothly as we drove along. It was a pleasant June evening, the sun just setting through the trees.

We turned onto the A-11 as darkness began to fall when "all hell broke loose." The car chilled noticeably, rapidly becoming colder. Most alarming, the steering wheel did exactly as I was told—it took on a life of its own, moving erratically.

"Look!" exclaimed Mrs Macdonald. I must confess my stomach turned as she held her hands lightly above the steering wheel. The car appeared to be steering itself. I have never witnessed anything quite like this before or since.

"Hold on to it!" I said to her. The A-11 is a very busy road, even at night and not one to be treated with disrespect. Then the car's lights commenced their strange behaviour. The lights flashed—not simply on and off, but up and down in intensity, bright, dim, excessively bright, turned off, dimmed again— flickering across the spectrum as if they were trying to show how clever they were! It was truly astounding to see. Cars coming towards us pulled over and stopped, their occupants frozen in amazement at what they saw. One driver even visibly rubbed his eyes like an awestruck child. We managed to steer the car over to the grass beside the road and turn off the engine.

It is important to understand that for psychic phenomena to occur, the presence of a "medium," albeit even one unconscious of his or her participation in the event, such as Mrs Macdonald, is absolutely necessary. It was clear to me that Mrs Macdonald was a natural psychic. I had become aware of that in our first moments of meeting, viewing as I always do in such circumstances, the information revealed by the colours of her aura. Her untrained sensitivity was out of control as a consequence of her postnatal depression and fluctuating emotions, her child being only a month or so old. This, for me, was the first key factor in the story—her own psychic energies having caused the disruption. She was psychically over active, too "open" to invisible presences.

Making the connection with John at that point lit her up like a psychic pinball machine, affecting all around her, especially the electrical equipment on the car. Temperature changes are usual around powerful psychic events indicating rising psychic activity, though this was rather exceptional. Furthermore, John was neither floating around there waiting for her, nor was he causing the problem. It was the location that triggered in her the strong emotions linked to memory of his death. This generated strong psychic energies in her, so that in her open psychic state, she became aware of him as he was thinking of her from his new world.

The second key was the location itself. It is also the site of a powerful ley-line, part of the earth's energy system which can be dowsed effectively by a good dowser. Such striking phenomena are often linked to this grid of power and sensitives are often affected by it, their already naturally heightened psychic awareness being further stimulated when they are physically close to its lines of force. Ancient sites of spiritual and social significance, such as standing stones, old churches, castles and the like are often located on this network. The older civilizations and more recent groups such as the Knights Templar were quite familiar with these invisible planetary forces.

My first thought in such circumstances is to locate the medium who is triggering the situation and to calm that individual down. I placed my hand in front of her body above her solar plexus, the area near to the stomach that is the focus for much of our primitive and uncontrolled psychic experience. This healing act was sufficient.

A gentle stillness descended upon all of us, especially Mrs Macdonald. The entire atmosphere changed. The air felt warm again, losing its uneasy chill and all was bathed in a beautiful tranquility. I was then aware of a young man, appearing briefly near to us, smiling and touching his heart as if to say 'It's okay. I love you still and I am fine.' He then vanished, the car lights ceased their frantic dance and there was a deep sigh of relief in us all. Our young visitor was John, an angel looking through on those he loved.

Mrs Macdonald never experienced these problems again.

Dave visits his old house

I was called to investigate another strange occurrence not far from my home, in a part of the town where there are some older houses, standing close to the former site of St. Saviours' Hospital. The ruins are all that remain of a large former medieval complex of buildings.

A young lady, I shall call Jane, called regarding her increasing concern about the noises in her house. She heard footsteps up the stairs and around the bedrooms, doors closing for no apparent reason, lights flickering spontaneously, and the strong sense of a presence around the house. She experienced a "cold spot" outside one of the bedrooms where the air felt untypically chilly as she walked through it. There was also a feeling of a "presence" throughout the house. Furthermore, her next-door neighbour was experiencing similar problems.

The house was a neat, older property along a busy road. Jane greeted me at the door, an attractive, intelligent young lady who was a teacher in a local primary school. She ushered me into the hallway, where immediately I became aware of a male angel, visiting us from another world. His presence was indeed strong, but in no sense was it malevolent or even slightly intimidating, as Jane had feared it was. We often initially fear things we don't understand or are strange to us, especially the occult, invisible forces around us when we become awakened to their interaction with us.

The house was being renovated—quite tastefully from what I could see—by Jane and her husband. They had been working hard to complete this reconstruction. I was to learn they were trying to start a family but had difficulties with her becoming pregnant. She was involved in a fertility programme, which made her anxious and a bit desperate. It was clear to me, that whatever psychic and spiritual events were manifesting, Jane was the medium through which it was happening.

We moved into her sitting room to discuss the situation, allowing me to assess things more thoroughly. We then moved through the house and our visiting angel followed, watching what we were doing. I began to communicate with him.

His name was Dave, and he was the previous owner of the house. In fact, he had been born in the house and lived in it all his life, alone in his latter years. He was pleased the house was being smartened up and liked the idea of a child entering the world there—which he told me would happen and that Jane would become pregnant in due course.

It is worth noting here, that when we no longer inhabit our earthly body after its death, we no longer experience the limits in awareness imposed on us by its dense nature. With the more elevated perspective we develop, we are able, to a greater degree, to look along life's timeline a little farther to see what those still on earth have already created in their future by their current and past thoughts and actions. In that state we are able to prophesy what is most likely to happen in the near future. However, nothing in life is absolutely certain. We have free will, largely restricted to our reactions to events and our subsequent behaviour. These factors in turn determine the course of our future, but many things are extremely likely to happen as effects eventually follow the earlier causes we have already set in place. It is reaping and sowing, or what is termed karma. Dave could see this was so regarding Jane's longed-for pregnancy. Dave indicated the bedroom he had occupied when he had been in the house and told me he was happy it was the room being prepared as a nursery. Jane was most surprised when I mentioned this to her.

"How do you know that?" she asked, looking a little startled.

"Dave told me," I responded. "He is very happy with the idea and loves what you are doing to the house."

"I thought he was angry about the changes!"

"No," I said, "quite the opposite."

It is not unusual for psychic energies to be released when an older building is being altered, or even demolished. Buildings are like blotting paper, psychically speaking. The memories and events of the past are in some way absorbed into them and their energy field, and they are sometimes disrupted and propelled out into the surrounding atmosphere on the site. Someone who is naturally sensitive, especially enduring a difficult emotional time as Jane was, would pick up on such things.

Dave was not an angry ghost or confused spirit. He was a soul, a true angel with a message. Now in the higher life, he still occasionally made contact with us here because of his attachment to the place in which he grew up and which held so many memories for him. After all, we all like to visit places from our earlier lifetime, to reminisce and relive past times—the happy, the sad, and the poignant moments that shape us and make us who we are. That continues for a time after death.

In fact, the cold spot was actually where Dave's body was found. He died suddenly and was discovered by his neighbour, who, incidentally, still lives next door and is also subject to Dave's visits.

"He wants to say he is fine and he wishes to help you take care of the house," I told Jane.

She looked relieved and I explained what I thought was going on here—her heightened sensitivity to spiritual presences helped Dave realize she was aware of him, thus encouraging his desire and effort to communicate, literally to say "Hello."

I informed Dave that, whilst his visits were welcome, he must be careful not to disrupt or intrude in the family life now unfolding in the house—a house that was no longer his. He was happy with that, smiled and left us for a while.

Shortly afterwards, the next-door neighbour called at the door and joined us in the sitting room for a cup of tea. She began to recount her own story, one of noises, footsteps and flashing light bulbs. Even her husband's hi-fi had ceased to work after the last bout of these phenomena. Dave joined us again. He said a 'Thank you' to the neighbour for helping him when he was here on earth and for sometimes bringing him cooked meals and cakes as a gift. She had been concerned about him living alone and had been a good friend to him.

"He is pleased to see you making fruit scones again," I told her. She was quite surprised.

"He says he popped into your kitchen to watch you. You always made lovely cakes—but he is most pleased about the scones!"

"That is amazing!" she replied, "I have just bought a new mixer, and today, for the first time in ages, I made some scones. How does he know that?"

"Just watching an old friend," I replied. "And he is sorry about the light bulbs."

Apparently, during one flashing light episode, a light bulb blew rather loudly, startling both her and her husband. She smiled and then laughed; always a good sign in such circumstances. Laughter is a great disperser of anxiety and troublesome psychic energies. I will relate some stories in Chapter 8 about angel visitors illustrating that we don't lose our sense of humour when we pass on.

I gave healing to both ladies and a prayer of blessing to the house, and then went to the neighbour's house to do the same.

While I was there I touched the hi-fi whilst I was still in a healing mode. It immediately lit up and functioned, continuing to do so for another year, until, I learned later, 'old age' led to its retirement!

Dave was never a problem again, even if Jane was occasionally aware of him, bringing his warm presence to greet her by the front door. And soon afterwards, Jane discovered she was pregnant. Her lovely baby daughter now happily occupies Dave's old room.

CHAPTER 4

Young Angels

When a loved one dies and leaves us here on the earth, regardless of what we believe about an afterlife, our sense of loss can remain with us for a considerable time. For some the pain and tears takes years to disappear completely, if ever.

I remember the physical pain my own Mum experienced in her last days and how relieved I was for her when she finally died. But even after all these years I miss her, with all her idiosyncrasies and her sometimes irritating ways. I miss her because, after all, she was my Mum.

When the anniversary of a loved one's passing comes around, our thoughts are often drawn to them, to the memories of those times we shared together, the ups and downs, the good times and not-so-good, the laughter and the sadness. We may discover their old watch in a drawer, or look at their photograph, and feel them smiling at us, or reminding us of the precious moments now gone. Or perhaps a song from our childhood on the radio stirs up memories of our Mum who sat with us for hours as we built an imaginary world with our toys, of her reading us our favourite book and talking with us about our dreams of what we would be when we grew up.

At times of death and birth we are drawn away from our usual day-to-day perspectives, our hearts filling with gratitude for those things that really matter, especially being loved and cared for by those who have been taken away from us.

But the death of a child is different, especially a young child. It can be the most devastating experience those left behind will ever encounter. They have their hopes and visions for the future before them, which we share with them, dreaming of all they can achieve in life. There is so much ahead for them to do and then, as it appears to us, unfairly their lives are taken away. They die, sometimes painfully, but usually with a level of fortitude and acceptance that often belies their tender age and that may put us older people to shame.

In my work with the surviving loved ones of those who die young, I have observed that these children are often less daunted by the prospect of death than those they leave behind here on earth. This was confirmed in the work of the late Dr. Elizabeth Kubler-Ross. It reveals that young souls seem able to cope with death better than adults do, often exhibiting a greater awareness of the essential transience of this life and its part in the larger scheme of things. Perhaps it is that they remember their pre-birth origins more clearly than we older, life-worn adults do, and know intuitively that they return at death to better things. William Wordsworth beautifully expressed this in his poem, "Ode: Intimations of Immortality from Recollections of Early Childhood," that as babes we are born "But trailing clouds of glory do we come, From God, who is our home..."

I can confirm the reality of a better place after death from my own youthful experience. I briefly "died" from a lightning strike when aged seventeen. I have never experienced before or since the immense sense of freedom I felt as I floated high above my unconscious body. If that is death then, it is certainly not to be feared.

Most children have imaginary friends. Being naturally more psychically alive, they are often aware of other dimensions when they are small. However, this materially focused world we live in often closes this awareness down, so we lose contact with these higher worlds along with much of the knowledge, magic and sense of true belonging they bring to us. The "fairy lights" in my post-war London garden and the beautiful bell-like sounds that accompanied them are as vivid to me now as they were to me as a young child. I can see and hear them now as I did then.

A young angel visits his mother

I visit the delightful Swiss village of Sennwald several times a year, to work and see clients. It is a beautiful location, surrounded by mountains and hills, and is close to the River Rhine, which forms a natural border with Liechtenstein. It was a cold autumn day, matching the mood of a new client I was to meet. She was the mother of a young boy who had recently died. The young woman entered my consulting room and sat quietly opposite to me. She looked nervous and was close to tears.

She told me that her son had died and she partly blamed herself. He had suffered from leukemia and the little lad had undergone difficult treatment involving a considerable amount of chemotherapy, debilitating and weakening him. She told me she believed this treatment had been more responsible for his death than his illness, and she wished, with hindsight, that she and her husband had stopped it when his health rapidly deteriorated.

Normally, before a clairvoyant session such as this, I prefer to know nothing about the clients and their circumstances. However, as they are often a little nervous about what is going to happen—it is a very strange experience for many and they simply don't know what to expect—we frequently exchange a few words to break the ice and put them at ease, as I did on this occasion. Should I feel they are giving me too much information, or beginning to mention issues which may pertain to the work I am about to do for them, I stop them politely, explaining why: that psychics and clairvoyants are often accused of feeding back to people what they have already deduced from clever questioning. I asked her to tell me no more than her first few words, whilst I explained what I was about to try to do for her, and see what angel contacts I could make.

Very quickly, I became aware of a lady, a nice pleasant soul who began to communicate with me.

"Do you know someone in the next world, someone who has passed on, who was called Tildi or Tilda?" I asked my client.

Matilda, or Tildi as she was called, was an aunt of this lady, a much-loved caring soul who had died some years earlier. Tildi gave me one or two other pieces of personal information, which my client acknowledged were correct.

Then she said, "I have brought someone to see you." A little boy gradually appeared, holding Tildi's hand. He then moved close to my client, putting his arm around her.

"I can feel that," she said as she gently shivered.

I told her that a little boy had put his arm around her and I was pretty sure it was her son, but I couldn't be absolutely certain at that point. Then I heard the name Andri, which was her son's name. He said it was nobody's fault that he died. His mother wept on hearing this.

Then Andri told her, "I love you, Mum and Dad and Issy (his sister). I love you all. Tell Dad I still go up the mountains with him."

He showed me his bicycle he loved to ride when he had been healthy and well. Andri had been an outdoor child when on earth, enjoying the marvelous countryside around his home. He also showed me in vivid pictures how he had loved to walk in the mountains, but when he became ill it was more and more difficult for him so his father had to carry him up on their final journey together.

Then he said, "Martin," which was his father's name. Coincidentally, though not to me, the feast day of St. Martin, Martinmass, was occurring that weekend. The family was planning a party.

"I shall be at the party," Andri said to me.

"He is showing me a cake," I told his mother. "He loved your cakes!"

Andri had been very close to his sister Issy. She was, at the time of our meeting and unbeknown to me, involved in a project at school studying squirrels. Her bedroom was filled with pictures and drawings of our little furry friends.

"He can see the squirrels in his sister's room," I told his mother. "Andri thinks she is doing well at school."

He could obviously see from his world the progress Issy was making. The young mother was delighted. She laughed. Happier tears now joined the tears of grief still flowing down her cheeks and she became more relaxed. She began to feel, she told me, that however tragic and painful her loss had been, her son was still somewhere around, still existed, and that one day she would see him again. Andri showed me a few more personal things that his mother understood and recognised. She also realised that he was now free of pain and suffered no more, and that he could now run up a mountain again, albeit in another world.

"Keep talking to my photograph," were his parting words—something he had watched his mother do each day, he said.

It was a powerful healing meeting. His mother now could "feel" his presence as many of us do when we realise we have been touched, lovingly, by those in another world. Andri would no doubt visit his mother often now that contact had been made.

A young man's message to his family—and to me

For those of us left behind, the emotional pain is equally intense when a slightly older, yet still youthful life leaves us. Once, I was working at a large public meeting with the celebrated psychic artist Coral Polge. Coral was also an accomplished medium who could use her artistic gifts to draw, with remarkable accuracy, the images of those seeking to communicate. One of these images she drew in this session was of a young man who wanted his family to know that he had survived death and still existed in another world.

None of his family were attending the meeting, but, fortunately, two of his neighbours were there who had known him and his family well and were able to identify his image. He had died in a motorcycle accident at the age of nineteen. It is worth mentioning here that no angel will bring a message unless there is someone present who may understand it, and know whom it is that brings it. There has to be a connection. It would be pretty pointless otherwise.

As Coral began to draw his picture, using a transparency on an overhead projector, he revealed his death in some detail to me, showing a picture of his much loved motorcycle and asking to be remembered to his Mum and Dad and his sister, and, as always, to give them his love and let them know he was okay in his new world. He wanted his sister to know that he was aware she was planning her wedding and that he was delighted for her. He also complained in a light-hearted manner how there won't be any bacon sandwiches at the reception. We were told that this was his favourite snack. The neighbours knew of this penchant of his and confirmed it with me.

The young soul then seemed to change in appearance. He suddenly began to radiate a bright golden-white light, which grew stronger and stronger until it was almost unbearable for me to view.

"There" he said to me. "You always wanted to see what the light of a soul was like, so here it is."

This was perfectly true. My studies of the human aura had failed to reveal this to me clairvoyantly until this moment and somehow he knew of my failed efforts.

"Bright, isn't it? And I am what you'd call an old soul!"

This statement referred to the belief held by many that those who die young are souls who have visited the earth many, many times, in various lives and guises. They are called old souls, who know before they are born into this life they will die young, to some good, if even mysterious, greater purpose. My great granny would often say, "The good die young." But when a very young child dies, it is even more poignant when they communicate to let us know they still exist.

Do children get older in the next world?

A question, which often arises from such sessions is, "Do children remain children in the next world when we move to the next life?" It's a question that does not lead to easy answers. I will discuss it more in later chapters when I recall some insights as to what we may do, for a while, when we move on to the next life. My experience over many years suggests that when we pass over and then return to contact those still here, that we come as they would recognise us. Coral Polge, the psychic artist whom I mentioned in the preceding story, told me how she noticed that communicating spirits often appeared looking younger than when they died, sometimes considerably so. I have noticed this on a few occasions, but as a general rule it is not necessarily true of my own experience. Most appear looking much as they did in the time just before they died.

Dr. Ian Pearce, a local physician who sadly passed on many years ago, wrote the book, *One Man's Odyssey,* related how, when he made contact with his daughter after her death as a teenager, she returned as the daughter he had known and loved, her words and dialogue being very much what one would expect from a loving teenage daughter when speaking to her beloved father. However, over the many sessions Ian had with a medium, his daughter began to change the nature of the messages, the content becoming more and more sophisticated. She explained to him that she was no longer a child, but had to make contact as that young girl initially, so he could more easily identify her. As time went by and the communication developed, she revealed that she was no longer his young daughter but a much greater soul—a different being entirely. That part of her experience had ended.

As visiting entities often explain, they are not constrained by the same time frame that we on earth experience and their contact with us does not hold them back or slow their progress in their new world. They contact us out of love and concern, freely so.

Comfort from a very young angel

Sometimes, the young angels who bring their messages are indeed very young as was the child involved in this next case. A young woman came to see me primarily for a healing treatment. She travelled up from London with a friend who knew me and had suggested I could help her. The woman was very distressed when she entered my office. Within a few moments, it became clear that she was grieving from the loss of a child who had died in the womb in the woman's eighth month of pregnancy. It had been a difficult time, and because of medical complications, she was concerned that she would never conceive again. This would have been her first child, and, she feared, her only one.

I reassured her that the baby she lost was fine now and existing in another world. During this time, a bright light appeared beside her, accompanied by one or two others. This I often see when clients ask me if they will ever have children. These lights, I have learned, are the lights of unborn souls who may incarnate through the individual at some time in the future.

This first light was the soul of the child who had died. I couldn't hear the name his parents had given to him, but it was clear to me that this was the light of a soul who had tried to be born as a boy, but failed to arrive. He told me very little, except that he would eventually be born through her so she need not worry. He continued to show me the other souls who would join him in her family in the coming years. His next comment to me was a little surprising.

"I'll be a girl next time!"

Sure enough, the prediction proved correct. A couple of years later, this young woman gave birth to a healthy daughter, followed in due course by two more girls. They all continue to thrive, more than sixteen years later. Why he then came back to the earth as a she is an interesting question; one that I cannot answer simply. Research and experience has revealed to me that we have many lives here on this planet, incarnating in both male and female bodies. Perhaps the tasks he wished to accomplish in his next life were best experienced as a woman. But back he came and is now a beautiful teenage girl called Isabel.

Tom

I met young angel, Tom, at the same time I met his mother, although I didn't know his name until later. I felt someone riding a small tricycle around my chair. I couldn't see who it was but I could certainly feel it. A little cycle bell rang out and then suddenly there was a loud bang and a cracking sound. It was clear to me that this was a little boy who had somehow sustained an injury whilst riding his trike.

I then learned that he indeed had an accident on his tricycle. What had seemed a minor bang to his head precipitated a freak brain injury from which he died a few days later.

All I was able to hear at first was, "I'm fine, Mum. I really am," followed by a large letter T, then an O written in the air in front of me. I told my client what I saw.

"It's Tom," his mother exclaimed with tearful excitement. "It's him."

He then blew a kiss and left us. The atmosphere calmed from the child-like exuberance that had dominated these few moments, to a peaceful quietness. This was followed by a smell of lavender and the appearance of the face and the body of an older woman. Holding the hand of the little boy, she impressed me with the thought; "He's with me now."

She removed her wedding ring as if to hand it to my client, pointing at her hand and also offering her tea and fruitcake. The older woman was the client's grandmother, whose wedding ring she now possessed and was wearing at the time. Grandmother had also been a fine cook, renowned for her cakes, especially her traditional fruitcakes.

"That's my Nan!" Tom's mother explained. "I really loved her and she died just before Tom was born, so she didn't know him."

"She does now," I replied.

This visit helped Tom's mother considerably in coping with her loss and I suspect it was good for Tom, too. And why the lavender? This was from the lavender bags Tom's mother used to make with her Nan, to place among her linens in her home.

She told me that her Nan's house always had the light perfume of this lavender whenever you opened the door.

Perfumes and childhood smells carry powerful memories for us and are often the calling cards of those angels who come to see us—a sudden wafting of a deceased loved one's favourite toilet water, or the cakes we made as a child, baking in the oven—simple, yet poignant thoughts that help our minds travel back and recall those past times and those we spent our precious moments with.

And Henry

Marlis has studied with me for some years, including regular appointments for guidance to help with her spiritual and general life direction. At the end of a recent session with her, a young boy appeared, announcing himself first as Henry and then, more correctly, as Heinrich. He somehow seemed to struggle with his words as he spoke to me, revealing a speech impediment he had suffered from during his short life. Marlis had worked with him and taught him, helping with his difficulties, especially his communication problems. She knew him well.

"He died earlier this year," she told me, somewhat surprised, yet delighted he had come through to let us know he had survived death and seemed to be fine.

"Tell Mother I like the rose; I have been watching her," Heinrich said to me. This comment puzzled Marlis, but she said she would pass the message on to his mother. The next day, Marlis called explaining she had spoken to Heinrich's mother. She told me that at the time Heinrich came to us, his mother was in her garden, tending to the rose bush that both she and her son had planted together. It was "their rose" and she was pruning it for the autumn, the last blooms having faded. She was very moved by this simple, yet significant message, given by her son, through a complete stranger. That night, she later reported, she felt a deep, relaxing warmth inside her, something that she had not experienced for months. For the first time since Heinrich's death, she slept deeply and contentedly.

This experience changed his mother's life. Since then she has been to see me on several occasions, and attended some of my courses. The last time I saw her, the once sad young woman glowed with confidence.

CHAPTER 5

Famous Names

⌒⬪⌒

*F*ew things strain credibility more, in my opinion, than mediums and psychics claiming they are in contact with the souls and spirits of famous individuals who are now in the higher life. When an eminent being has communicated through me from the next world, I have strongly advised the client against public disclosure, certainly for the time being. This is largely to avoid ridicule for them, and also not wishing to detract from the importance of the message given at the time.

I recall one headline in a less than reputable newspaper, which read, "Psychic has message from lonesome Elvis." Someone, somewhere, possibly seeking publicity or money (a common theme among psychics needing to be famous) had decided that Elvis Presley's spirit had visited her, giving her messages for the whole world to hear. Not only were the messages in themselves rather trite with no real significance to the general public, but also why Elvis Presley's spirit should have randomly visited a woman in a bungalow in Lancashire, England, I couldn't fathom. I am always a little suspicious of such claims. You'd have thought Elvis would at least try the Dalai Lama first!

As the following cases reveal, I have discovered over the years that when famous people come through in sessions with clients it is not an opportunity for me to make headlines in the press, but, as in contacts of every kind, to support the client or his or her family in some often unusual way. Or perhaps the intent is to point the client in a direction that may help him or her find evidence or information they are seeking related to an important project they are pursuing. Thankfully, such work I have done with clients has not been the subject of any silly media story. It is included here as relevant information for the reader and to illustrate another aspect of angel contact.

When it first happened to me that a well-known figure appeared during a consultation, I confess to experiencing a mixture of embarrassment and disbelief. But again, they were people who, for one life at least, were famous and despite all their success or wealth, they experience life much as we with a less public profile do. They have the same highs and lows and eventually leave this life through death as everyone must do. And if the messages they bring are meaningful and useful to those still living on earth, whether they knew them or not, then I think, why not?

I feel privileged that part of my life involves being asked to support difficult causes, causes that sometimes involve battles to establish the truth as the next two stories illustrate.

One famous angel visitor was a great surprise to me, and her appearance in my little office initially challenged my ideas, particularly in relation to souls who died not ten or twenty years ago, but nearly two centuries or more back. However, over some years of continuous contact with this soul, which is itself the subject of a book being written by the client mentioned in the story, the reason for this angel visit became clear to me and the first meeting is of sufficient merit to be included in these pages.

It began when a woman named Anne called to make an appointment. She had been referred to me by a medium who worked at the College of Psychic Studies in London. This medium was unable to help Anne at the time but she had previously consulted me herself, and thought I was the person Anne should see. I was told that Anne thought she was receiving psychic messages, but from whom, she was not sure. They came via a mysteriously moving milk jug that was in her possession. It was part of a Dresden china tea set Anne's late father had given to her and the jug would move unaided to the front of the display cabinet in which it was stored no matter how often it was removed to the back of the shelf. Naturally, Anne wanted to know what was going on. Was she imagining it or deluding herself? She was advised by the other medium that a visit to me might help clarify her situation, so a date was arranged and Anne came to see me.

She wished to determine the reason for her psychic experience, so I began to do a sketch of her aura colours. The arrangement of the coloured light in the human aura is a tool I use frequently to assess the nature of individuals, their overall development and the spiritual and psychic structures they have within them.

Anne's aura revealed that she was both artistic and strongly psychic. (I discovered much later that Anne had been a fine artist in her youth, winning a place to study at the Royal Academy, London.) What happened next was startling, even for me. I could see Anne's husband, Henry, in her aura. He was busy researching, wading through documents relating to family history and some mysterious work of art. I had not yet met Henry, who, at the time of my meeting with Anne, was waiting for her outside in their car.

Anne was surprised when I told her that I saw the research Henry was doing, and at the same time, pleased that I should see this, whilst ostensibly viewing her and her own issues. It is not uncommon that a client's family and close friends may feature in their own reading. The aura is a window into the life of the subject, often revealing many aspects of the past, present and future.

First, Anne's father communicated, admitting responsibility for moving the jug. He had tried to get her attention so that her curiosity would be aroused to investigate further. Phenomena such as objects moving mysteriously around the house are not uncommon when angels seek our attention.

Then came the moment I shall never forget. A young woman appeared in period dress, dating back to the late 1700s. She was quite articulate when she communicated to me, indicating she was related to Henry. She said she was called Jane and wanted to help them in their quest. She continued by telling me that they were correct to search these records and all would be proved in time.

Then she said directly to me, "You didn't like my book when you read it!"

The visiting angel in question was the author, Jane Austen. (I had been made to read her novel, *Emma*, as a twelve year-old and had found it less than interesting!) Henry was a direct descendant of Jane's brother, Edward, and possessed the only existing full-length oil painting of Jane. The National Portrait Gallery in London had once sought this painting, with what many experts consider to be an excellent provenance, for purchase as it is, obviously of enormous significance. Owned at that time by Henry's father, he declined to sell it, wishing instead to keep it in the family home. It had been accepted that the subject of the painting was indeed Jane Austen and that was not in dispute at that time. It was thought to have been painted by the artist, Zophany, and the date of its production was also accepted to be around 1788 when Jane was fourteen years old.

However, in more recent years, one critic began to question the authenticity of the work and launched a rather unpleasant campaign to discredit it, alluding to the style of dress worn by the painting's subject as being early 1800s and so could not possibly be a young Jane Austen. Experts with knowledge of period dress have subsequently disproved this objection, but my work over the years in respect of this painting suggests the art world is a strange one where opinions often matter more than facts. It seemed that Jane, and indeed her family and the real artist, Ozias Humphry, were trying to help Henry and Anne put the matter to rights. Humphry was a contemporary of his more illustrious friend, Zophany, and began to go blind in the late 1700s. If he painted the picture, as recent forensic evidence suggests he did, then it could not have been done in the early 1800s, as some critics have erroneously claimed to support their opposing view.

In a subsequent session Edward Knight, Jane's brother, also appeared to us. He discussed his diaries, which I had seen Henry busily checking at the beginning of the session. It was the second of many meetings over a period of some years with Henry and Anne. Gradually, information and guidance has been given to us until, at the time of writing, the denouement of the matter looks to be close at hand. Jane's insistence that eventually, "The painting will validate itself," is about to be seen to be true—thanks to much research, guidance from Jane herself, and a recent excellent portrait cleaning and restoration, revealing much that was hidden: and through the use of advanced digital photographic technology and forensics, which Jane suggested we should use.

In this process, infrared and ultraviolet techniques revealed the artist's logo, the date (1788) and the name, Austen, along with Godmersham, an estate in Kent where this portrait and that of her brother, Edward, were produced. Edward, in fact lived there after his adoption by the Knight family. And in an old photographic plate of the portrait, stored in the Heinz Library in London, simple techniques carried out by a forensic science company have also revealed not only the name Jane Austin, and the date on the front of the painting, but also the signature of the artist himself—Ozias Humphry.

These are a few of the highlights of an unfolding story, one that has split expert opinions of Jane Austen scholars in UK and America. However, with the help of the lady herself, Miss Austen, and others now in the next life, the story is nearing its conclusion. My first session with Anne opened the door not only to regular contact with the soul or spirit of this famous author, but also her sister, Cassandra, the painter, Ozias Humphry himself, Edward Knight, her brother, Colonel Thomas Austen, Jane's cousin of whom she was very fond, and her uncle, Francis Austen, a famous judge of the time. While Jane herself was the main communicator, the others appeared from time to time with additional pieces of information to support us in our quest, for a quest is what it has become.

Another aspect of the communication that may be interesting here to relate, involved Jane's sister, Cassandra Austen. In one dialogue Cassandra appeared, telling me that she was pregnant when her fiancé died in the Caribbean. We were surprised by this admission, particularly as there seemed to be no official record of this claim anywhere to be found. However, Cassandra was most insistent.

"I was pregnant—and I had a child," she told me.

I realize that such an assertion may upset many Austen fans and scholars, especially as we had no physical proof to support the claim. However, she was insistent that in our searches we would find some support for this story. And sure enough, we did.

It was sometime later when another article about the painting appeared in the *London Times* newspaper. It largely supported the claim that the identity of the subject of the portrait was Jane and raised fresh publicity on the matter both in England and elsewhere. A week or so later, Henry Rice received a letter from a man living in London. He had read about the painting and had a story that he thought, while not especially connected to the portrait, Henry might find interesting. (The newspaper article mentioned how we had searched in France for a portrait of Cassandra, which we believe still exists, undiscovered as yet. While I was at the centre of this search, visiting Vence near Nice, the area where we suspect it may be, I asked not to be mentioned publicly at that point in the story. My involvement is now more widely known.)

In his letter, the man described how, as a young boy, his mother had told him a story. It was a family secret, handed down over many generations until he was its last remaining custodian. He was told that he was descended from the illegitimate daughter of Cassandra Austen. Considering he knew nothing of my 'conversations' with her, this was remarkable.

Our visitors have given us much to reflect upon and valuable guidance as we seek recognition for this portrait. Thus far, they have been correct every time.

Archie Rice calls

Famous angels are not always supporting a cause or fighting injustice, but simply come for the joy and fun of connecting with old friends.

This was the case in another surprising communication that occurred in a session in Kent while meeting with an older gentleman. I remember how smartly dressed he was and that he wore a flamboyantly patterned matching handkerchief and tie with a brightly coloured paisley design. This man had a noticeable presence one could sense. Observing his manner and dress I was not surprised to learn that he was an actor. I have seen many performers, writers and musicians over the years, some famous, some not so, although I didn't know or recognize him. However it was apparent he had performed many times in London's West End theatres and also in film and television.

As we sat together, first his departed mother came to us and gave him some personal information, largely concerning childhood memories of family holidays and his thespian qualities being evident to her, even when he was a boy. He understood perfectly, crying a little, but with tears of joy rather than sorrow. He removed his glasses, proceeding to wipe them rather theatrically, with his paisley handkerchief. He then smiled and said, "Thank you. That was a great help to me. She is okay, isn't she?"

"Of course she is," I reassured him.

Our meeting was coming to a close when quite suddenly, I experienced a rush of energy, like a strong, cool wind. Some immense, invisible figure had brushed past me. I could hear music, a song I recognized, but from where I didn't recall. The voice of a man became increasingly audible to me, a man who, in this life, must have clearly possessed an enormously powerful presence.

"Hello, Old Cock! Glad I caught you!" the angel said for me to communicate to my client.

My client's jaw dropped visibly when I repeated this to him. His eyes stared vaguely ahead for a few moments, as if in shock and briefly, I confess, I was a little concerned for him. But after letting out a little cry, then sobbing gently, he began to speak again.

"That's Larry—can you see him?"

Indeed I could! To my astonishment, before my eyes, appeared the unmistakable form of Sir Lawrence Olivier. He had been a great friend of this man. His words of greeting, I learned subsequently, were ones he used often. Our angel visitor laughed out loud. One could almost feel the room shake. He mentioned a play or two that they had done together and a few other pleasantries, then he started to sing the tune again, the one that had announced his visit to us.

I hummed the tune I could hear.

"It was when he played Archie—Archie Rice," my client exclaimed.

This was a reference to Sir Lawrence's portrayal of the character Archie Rice in John Osborne's play, *The Entertainer*, which had also been made into a film with his then wife, Joan Plowright, as his co-star. He lifted the straw boater hat he was wearing, said, "Cheerio, Old Cock," and left us. It was no doubt a brief, but powerful visit from a remarkable talent, still performing in the higher life.

A musical giant brings some clues

The preceding stories in this chapter demonstrate that the link between the client and the visiting entity was fairly straightforward. They were essentially personal. Anne and Henry were connected to Jane Austen by ancestry and Sir Lawrence briefly contacted an old friend he had known well.

However, the next angel visit was purely a professional one, not personal.

The client, Angela, consulted me for a specific purpose. She was a musician who felt she was being guided in some unusual manner in her work and her research. A concert pianist and university lecturer, she had a particular mission in her life that, despite her tenacity, she was finding difficult to see through. Just as Anne and Henry had been battling with a small, yet vociferous group of opponents in the art establishment of this country, Angela had a similar issue in the world of classical music.

As she sat with me, my room filled with piano music, which I immediately recognised as Chopin. Then a backdrop of musical scores, notation and scribbles on sheets of music manuscript came into my vision, followed by a figure, again in period dress, trying to point out certain details on the sheets of musical notes, hanging like washing on an invisible clothes line behind Angela.

"I hesitate to say this," I remarked, "but I think we have a visit from the man himself—Chopin."

Angela smiled, the tension in her earnest expression draining away from her face. She lit up.

"I do hope that is true," she replied. "I need his help right now. I've often felt that he was around but then thought, no it's a delusion!"

Her mission concerned the playing and interpretation of the great master's work. Through her extensive research of Chopin's manuscripts and her own musical expertise and knowledge, she had come to the conclusion that many contemporary performances of Chopin's work were incorrect. Recent editions of his compositions, accepted as the norm, were actually not as he intended them to be, or as they would have sounded in his day. While I have reasonable musical knowledge, I didn't understand the subtleties of much of these conversations. I simply commented on what I could see clairvoyantly and what I heard, most of which Angela appeared to understand.

Through her lectures, recitals and CD recordings, she had sought to offer a different interpretation as to what we should really be hearing of the great man's compositions, how he intended them to be performed. And in so doing, she had encountered the wrath of many in the musical establishment who tried to dismiss her claims, and, worse still, sabotage her efforts to record, publicise, and distribute her work.

The resistance she encountered frustrated her, but the presence of Chopin in our sessions encouraged her. It was obvious that while he may not have agreed with every detail of her theories—occasionally he would indicate so by shaking his head as if to say "No!" Most of it he did endorse. When he disagreed, he would offer another phrase of music instead, usually shown to me as a picture of a piece of music manuscript or on other occasions as a phrase of music I could hear. He was trying to help her with interpretation of performance as well as a better structure for some of his compositions. During this, and one or two subsequent sessions, the great musical master pointed out many things, gave advice and answered as many questions.

While he, of course, had never known Angela personally, he was interested in her work and wished to support her as she followed her beliefs, seeking to unravel the truth. This is an important issue. As with Jane Austen, the communicators all want to encourage our research so the truth of the matter may be established, and to help those suffering some kind of injustice and even persecution for their convictions. Angela told me that one "mysterious" individual attempted to buy up the entire stock of one of her Chopin CDs rather than have them go on public sale. It is rather curious the lengths some may go to in order to stifle debate and conceal an opinion that differs from their own.

A brief period of illness slowed Angela's momentum for a while and we lost contact. But she reappeared in my office a couple of years ago, healthy and vibrant, with a renewed passion to continue her campaign, including the production and release of some new recordings. It was clear to me that Chopin continues to help and guide her, and one day, perhaps he will be watching her as she receives the acclaim she so richly deserves.

And an artist

In my psychic research concerning the portrait of Jane Austen, I went to Vence near Nice in France for a few days. This quaint French town had appeared to me earlier in clairvoyant visions. I saw it in great detail during my sessions with Henry and Anne in our efforts to locate the portrait of Jane's sister, Cassandra. Our research had led us to a Mrs Harrison, a member of a large, wealthy English community that lived among the famous artists of the day. She had owned a house in Vence, was a member of the Austen family and had possibly owned the portrait of Cassandra at one time. She also owned a large collection of paintings before she died and for a while had been a neighbour of Picasso as well as other talented artists.

My guidance suggested Mrs Harrison had certainly owned this picture and we were following various trails, both psychically and humanly inspired, to unearth it. I had seen in my earlier visions, the church in Vence, the recent renovations it had undergone, and a street or two in the town with some clarity, but the information was fragmented and Henry felt that I might have more luck if I visited the location for myself. After hours of walking around looking for clues and waiting to see if I received any further guidance on the matter, my feet were sore and I started to tire. It was a pleasant warm May evening and I decided to go to the town square to relax with a glass of wine and a cigar.

After making a bit of a fool of myself (and having a little fun at it!) trying to use my schoolboy French in a tobacconist shop, I found a comfortable seat outside a small cafe, sat down, and began to watch some locals as they played the French bowls game *petanque*, in the remaining sunshine. It was a happy, relaxed atmosphere and I was looking forward to some more delicious fish for my supper that was on offer at the small hotel where I was staying.

I felt someone sit down in the chair beside me and turned to smile and wish them a good evening. To my surprise, it was one of our angel visitors, a bearded bespectacled gentleman, dressed a little old fashioned, complete with walking stick and hat. His face was strangely familiar to me, but at that moment I couldn't summon up the name. I puzzled over this, racking my brain.

"I recognise you," I thought. "Who are you?"

At first, a few French words drifted into my head, but sadly, my limited linguistic skills failed to interpret what had been said. The figure smiled again at me and then clearly stated in English, "Matisse, young man. Henri Emile Matisse."

This was unmistakable. Matisse was an artist whose work I knew and admired. I had read about him many times in my years as an art teacher. Next, I heard. "Keep looking. Keep looking."

And he vanished as quickly as he came. I later discovered he also had been a regular visitor to Vence. He had lived there for a time and designed the famous local Rosaire Chapel. For some reason he had decided to make contact in that moment. As with many contacts in other countries, sometimes the visitor will use the language of his last life on earth and then, switch to English. I have experienced this many times in Europe.

Well, we did keep looking but financial and time constraints have limited our endeavours. We have yet to find Cassandra's portrait, but the promised flow of evidence to support and prove the authenticity of Jane's painting has been little short of astounding and encourages that quest to continue. Particularly interesting is the discovery of previously hidden marks and writing on the canvas, which I was told we would find. For those interested to read more I suggest they visit the website www.janeaustenriceportrait.com.

Perhaps this is what Matisse was trying to tell me: Keep looking. Keep looking. It has all certainly been worth looking for. We have far more help from our angel friends than we realize—even the famous ones.

CHAPTER 6

Suicides and Murders

⸻

*T*he majority of angel visitors that we clairvoyants see come to contact us in a happy, even sometimes playful frame of mind. There may be tears on both sides of the dialogue, so a box of tissues for clients is a must in any reading or appointment. Sometimes the medium may also feel the strong "choked" sensation in the throat that the communicators convey, with tears of joy, affection and healing, and a great sigh of relief that contact has been made.

Occasionally however, the situation is initially a little darker, where the passing from this life was the consequence of a bad accident, perhaps negligence of some kind. Or even more difficult for all involved, is when those who left this life through a suicide or a murder pay a visit.

"I'm not being punished for what I did"

The woman who came to me was not new to clairvoyance, readings or metaphysics. She had experienced psychic matters before and was interested in discovering more, especially about healing work, which she emphasized during her first appointment. Her name was Marion. Her facial expressions in response to what I said confirmed her growing interest: A smile one moment, then a puzzled look, an opened mouthed, "Oh, I know what that is. Yes, I know," and again would come another smile.

Then Marion's favourite grandmother announced herself with the sound of clicking knitting needles, followed by recollections of how Marion, as a child, sat with her learning to knit, sew, and crochet. These were ordinary things, not particularly interesting or unusual in themselves, but the kinds of evidential memories that help us confirm the identity of those communicating from the higher life now engaged in conversation with us. The activities we shared with them—happy, sometimes sad, yet always powerful memories describing intimate, personal moments we may have long forgotten.

The grandmother apologized for passing before Marion had arrived to see her. A severe stroke proved to be her last illness and her granddaughter was actually driving to her house when she died.

"I have someone who needs to speak to you. He's with me now."

Marion's expression immediately switched to sadness laced with fear. She seemed to know who this was before any identification was made. A man appeared, alongside the grandmother. As his presence with us strengthened, I could see that he was probably in his mid-forties when he passed on. He looked a little hesitant.

"It is all okay here. I am fine. I was not punished for what I did."

The man's name was Malcolm, Marion's husband. He was a rather tubby individual, who, in this life, had curly hair, red cheeks, big soulful eyes and wore spectacles. There was no hint of a smile on his face as he tried to convey his message to us.

"I'm sorry." He seemed to shake his head as I felt his words. "I understand now. I have not been punished, just helped to understand by beings in this world what I did, the consequences of it all."

Upon hearing these words Marion relaxed once more and a soft smile appeared across her face. Communications from angels always bring the energy of healing to their loved ones whatever circumstances surrounded the death.

After a pause, I saw him show me a picture of his daughters, who were still on the earth, living with their mother. He wanted to say 'sorry' to them, to cuddle them again. Malcolm had committed suicide some months earlier. Sadly, his relationship with Marion had broken down after many, many attempts to put it right. He admitted to not being an easy man to live with.

She said, "I loved him in a sense, but not deeply. I was not in love with him. He couldn't cope with that. He threatened to end his life and I didn't believe he would..."

Her voice faded away as she swallowed noticeably. He had apparently made many suicide threats over a long period; so distraught was he that the woman he loved had never really loved him. Malcolm showed me an image of a car and the smell of choking exhaust fumes seemed to fill the room.

"Was it in a car, with exhaust fumes?" I asked.

"Yes, it was. He did it in the forest and the police found him."

It was a deeply sad moment. Remorse was experienced in both worlds. They were both sorry for what had happened and despite the difficulties they had experienced in their relationship, they still cared for each other. He left us then and after a little more discussion, the session concluded. Marion was relieved. She felt she could move on with her life and was now convinced that Malcolm would progress too, albeit in another sphere of life, another world. She did admit, however, that she now wished she had tried more to make things work between them.

Such a contact is most revealing, teaching us that when individuals take their own lives in suicide, they are not punished and condemned to eternal damnation or some kind of purgatory, but rather aided by wiser souls to look at what they have done so they may seek to understand it. My experience tends to confirm this is true for everything we do, or have done here on earth. We are not judged, no matter what some religious dogma or current social morality may suggest is acceptable. Rather, we judge ourselves. At the very least, we evaluate our past actions for ourselves and are helped to do so, learning from them so we can grow, become wiser, and henceforth, better, more useful souls. Perhaps this is why we say those drowning may see their lives pass before their eyes as they approach death (an experience reported by some who have been rescued from drowning). It is for us to look at what we do and through these lessons, grow up, become stronger and know what it is that we might change in similar circumstances, should they come around again.

Malcolm didn't meet St Peter at the pearly gates (I've never heard any communicating angel tell me they have either!) but with assistance, he encountered himself and deduced his own lessons from what he saw and what he had done.

A pair of shoes brought his parents peace

A local family suffered a similar sadness—a family I knew something of, as our children had attended the same schools. I'd heard how one of their sons, with no apparent warning, took his life by hanging himself in his bedroom. It was not an accident. He'd left a brief note saying he was sorry. The parents, who were intelligent, devoutly religious people, received some succour from the priests at their church, but were still in deep grief at the loss of a son they adored. They knew something of my work and came around for a chat one afternoon. Since I knew a little of the story, I did my best to help them. The father was particularly in a deep state of grief.

He asked me over and over again if his son was at peace. I assured him that their son would be fine, looked after and loved in his new world. I told them both some stories from my past experience that I felt would help to reassure them.

The young man then appeared to me. I hadn't known him especially well, but the description of him I gave—his dress and one or two little details—seemed to confirm to them that it was him I saw. Again, I offered words of comfort to his parents, confirming he had settled well in his new world. Then I noticed that he wasn't wearing any shoes. When I said this to his parents they were puzzled. Such simple things as this often have real meaning to those clients who are with me, but his "shoelessness" carried no significant meaning for them. After a little more conversation, they thanked me for my time and kindness and decided to leave. I was hoping that I had managed, in some way, to help them move forward in their lives and heal their pain if only a little.

As a last communication, the boy pointed to his feet, saying to me, "Tell Dad I like his shoes!" I could feel a cheeky smile radiating from his face as he spoke.

"They were his trainers," his father replied, looking down at his son's shoes he now wore, smiling and crying a little at the same time. "These were almost new. He bought them. That's why he had no shoes!"

These few words meant so much to them and contributed, in time, to peace coming into their lives, as well as that of their departed son.

"He didn't kill me"

I had never had occasion to consider deeply what happens to those who pass on who have been involved in murder, either as victim or perpetrator. It had been the subject for reflection of course, but there had never been any direct communication for me on the matter from angels, making any view I formed purely conjectural—until a visit by a young woman who lived locally came to see me for an aura reading. One is often asked about Judas Iscariot for example, implicit in the death of Jesus—if not exactly his murderer and ultimately, a suicide himself. And what about mass murderers and sadistic serial killers? I now feel confident a process of rehabilitation, loving help and self-realisation is in place for them all, as it is for the rest of us whose misdemeanors may have been less dramatic.

This young woman was concerned about her future path and wished to see if I could shed a little light on where she may go in her life in the times ahead. This I tried to do. I could also see there was sorrow and a little anger in her aura, but she wouldn't be drawn into a discussion when I mentioned it to her. "Can we leave that?" she said, a little abruptly, as I attempted to discover what the problems were.

She then said to me, "Is there anyone around? Anyone from the other side?"

This made me smile—the phrase "the other side" has a rather dated, almost humorous quality for me, shades of the medium in a darkened room, hands on table, eyes closed, asking in a séance, "Is anybody there?" It is all a bit Madame La La and I have a problem with certain jargon and some medium-speak language, which seems to proliferate amongst many clairvoyants.

So I looked and saw an older lady with her. From my descriptions we were able to recognise her as my client's grandmother. She then revealed that her grandmother had been murdered, having had what must have been a terrifying death.

"He didn't kill me!" the angel said. "It was somebody else, someone I didn't know."

My young client became very subdued. Then, with her eyes filling with tears, she said, "I knew he didn't. We all do. Is there anything we can do?" At this point I had no idea who "He" was, but it was soon to be revealed.

The angel went on to tell us it would be difficult. She had been murdered by a stranger she told us, yet her grandson, my client's brother, who had visited his grandmother shortly before the crime was committed, was suspected and eventually convicted. The family had always thought he was innocent, as he had maintained throughout his trial and his subsequent imprisonment. This was the issue I had seen in her aura but, initially at least, she was unwilling to discuss. The energy she felt as her grandmother appeared to us had touched her heart, as these things often do, and released some of the tensions connected with this awful family story. As I said earlier, tears often flow and words then follow.

"We are campaigning, looking at trying to get some kind of a review of the case or the verdict," she said, "but I don't think we'll get anywhere. We think he was set up, maybe by one of his friends of dubious character. He had a lot of them."

Her brother had been a drug user, had some financial problems and had previously borrowed money from his grandmother. In view of his past, including him having a quick temper, and the available evidence presented—he had no supported alibi—he was convicted of his grandmother's murder, as money was found to be missing, some of which was found on his person. But she had often given him a little cash, sometimes against her better judgement, realising he may use it to fuel his addictions. She had given this money to him on this occasion too, just as he claimed regardless of what the other evidence suggested. His grandmother's communications were quite clear. He was not her murderer.

Such a message from a troubled angel as she was leaves one feeling powerless. Who is going to believe the words of a clairvoyant, indeed in such a critical matter as this? It is frustrating to know he is still serving his sentence, persisting with his claim of innocence. I realize many do make such claims when convicted even though they are in fact guilty of the crime they so protest they never committed. But this was a sad and difficult communication that was unable to help his cause, or at least promote a review of the evidence—at least, not yet.

It makes one wonder how many people may be wrongly imprisoned around the world. I remain convinced the family is right.

How difficult must it be for this grandmother angel to witness what has happened to her grandson here on earth? One can only hope that justice will eventually be done.

CHAPTER 7

Angels in America

*W*hen I first embarked on clairvoyant and healing work it often included travelling to towns and cities throughout the UK and eventually abroad as my reputation for reliable work developed. I enjoy all this moving around, visiting different places and people. I have never sought work anywhere in particular—it has always been by invitation—and other than a few leaflets, my simple Internet website and some fairly successful books, I have never seriously advertised my work. I have simply relied on being summoned to wherever it is I am meant to be. It works well, if slowly at times, and one learns that popularity, and, indeed success, can be rather transient, as venues and clients come and go, my work with them finished.

These days, I have clients in countries around the world, many of whom I have never met face to face. I work with them over the telephone, through email, and lately Skype, as I slowly grasped the technological nettle. This works very well and enables me to help people in areas and countries who are too far away to see me at my home, although it is surprising what lengths some will go to—planes, trains, taxis, and staying in hotel rooms—just so they can have a brief face-to-face consultation. Such determination amazes me, and I must say that I find it rather humbling. However, meeting and working with someone in person is always preferable to me. Wherever I go, I find people are essentially the same. Underneath the social and cultural differences, we all have similar needs, the same dreams and hopes, fears and sorrows. A loved one passing from this life affects us all profoundly, whoever and wherever we are, whatever our beliefs may be. It is a powerful reminder of our own mortality and the fragile hold we have on our lives here.

USA call-in radio show with the "Curious Psychic"

I was once a studio guest on a phone-in radio show in Tacoma, Washington, near Seattle. It was a successful show with a great host. Her name was Shirlee Teabo, an accomplished American psychic who had her own weekly programme for two hours on Saturday mornings with her journalist sister, Jacquie Witherrite as co-anchor. They also had a weekly newspaper column called "The Curious Psychic," which discussed a range of spiritual and psychic matters, stories of interesting encounters and other metaphysical themes.

The programme was going very well. Occasionally I was asked to speak to one of the listeners who had phoned in, mainly to talk about their auras, the colours I saw, and any brief, pertinent message I had for them. The presenters were amazed that I could see someone's aura when they weren't even present in the room, but, as I mentioned, I often have to give advice over the telephone to a client thousands of miles away. In those circumstances, the aura is as clear to me as when the client is physically present.

On this particular day, all had gone along nicely. My stint was finished near the end of the first hour, when we took a longer break for commercials, the news and sports bulletins. I removed my headphones and stood up in the studio to make my farewells to Shirlee and Jacquie while we were off air for a few minutes.

"What are you doing now?" Shirlee enquired.

"I'm having a relaxing day, maybe going downtown to have a drink and a cinnamon bun! It's a free day today," I replied.

"Sit down!" she retorted, in a mock schoolmistress voice. "You're going nowhere. This switchboard is hot." Shirlee pointed to the contraption in front of her, lights flashing, indicating that the calls from her listeners were stacking up. Meekly, I did as I was summoned to do—Shirlee was a lovely though formidable woman. I replaced my headphones and requested another cup of tea from the studio staff.

"Girls!" Shirlee greeted the listeners as we went back on air, in grand theatrical style. "That lovely Englishman we had here before the break… well, we've tied him to the chair and he ain't going anywhere. We've got him for another whole hour!"

Recorded cheers and cat-calls then followed and I found the whole thing hilariously zany. A woman came on line shortly afterwards and asked to speak to the Englishman, her voice revealing her anxiety.

"My name is Kathy," she said softly. "Paul, what colours can you see in my aura?"

I described the powerful green light, which indicated to me that she had experienced considerable changes over the last year. A dark grape violet also highly visible revealed her sadness and heavy heart, from painful inner reflection, possibly due to loss or bereavement. While she was still clearly troubled, her sadness didn't appear to be linked to a recent passing. She confirmed this as correct, along with one or two other pieces of information I gave. However, such radio and T.V. phone-ins strictly ration a caller's airtime, and signals from the producer in my headphones told me to say goodbye as quickly and politely as possible since another caller waited.

"Paul," Kathy interrupted as I said goodbye to her, "is it possible to get an appointment to see you?"

"Leave your number before you ring off and we'll see what we can do," I replied. I had a trip to Mount St. Helens arranged to see the effects of the volcanic eruption there in the 1980s and another day or two of sightseeing, but no other appointments scheduled. I really felt I had to see her, so we arranged to meet one afternoon at the home of my friends in nearby Lakewood City.

Kathy was a bright, well-dressed middle-aged woman, who, I learned, was facing many decisions. She was quite alone with no one especially close to her whom she felt she could trust to give her sound objective advice. She felt a session with me might help her to get her thoughts straight and clear her mind a little. In our 45 or so minutes together I did the best I could for her and she noticeably relaxed, but I was aware we were not yet finished. Suddenly a man appeared, standing behind her. It was her deceased husband. Many of Kathy's concerns had centered on their relationship, its difficulties and his struggle with alcohol in the last years of his life. They had not been on good terms when he died, living separately for a while to see if things might improve between them.

He was wearing his Air Force uniform. His service years had been a time during which he flourished, winning many promotions. He was proud of his achievements, and rightly so. However, as with many who spend years in the military world with its camaraderie and clearly defined structures, a return to civilian life can sometimes prove difficult to cope with. That was when his problems with drinking began. He apologized to her for his excessive drinking and bad tempers, and also assuring her that from where he was he could see her solving many of the problems confronting her without much difficulty.

She was comforted enormously by this, shedding a tear or two as he continued to tell her that he no longer had the problems caused in his earthly life by alcohol or the "juice" as he put it. He mentioned the month of March, while showing me a huge bouquet of flowers. Kathy informed me that it was the anniversary month of their wedding and also his birthday.

As he made his farewells he told us, "I hope you like the photograph of me in my uniform!"

Kathy had difficulty with that. "Sadly, I have no photograph of him dressed like that. I know I don't," she replied.

She then left me, commenting how much she enjoyed the radio show and hoped we would meet again, although, as is often the case in my work, you rarely do.

A few days later Kathy called, rather excited, just before I left for my flight to London. She had just received a letter through the post from the sister of her late husband who lived in California. Accompaning the brief note was a photograph of him, resplendent in his uniform, just as I had seen him. Kathy's sister-in-law had been clearing out some old drawers and found the photo, which she felt Kathy would like to have as a memento of a man she loved and missed. Particularly interesting were Kathy's last comments to me. "And the date and time of the postmark on the envelope was that of the date and time of our meeting. He clearly knew something we didn't!"

Come to the barbecue!

On the other end of the telephone was a young woman concerned about her future and what she should do after completing her college studies. I was able to help her as we sifted through the ideas she had. The aura is a very useful tool for understanding the general makeup of an individual, especially discerning the kinds of roles and career they may flourish in. For some years now I have been retained by several companies to help them in, amongst other things, their staff selection processes at senior management levels. This was featured a while back in the *London Sunday Times* newspaper business section.

A voice then called me. It was one of her angels.

"It's Ken," he called out. "Tell her I still love her and look over her from time to time."

I heard some gentle sobs on the other end of the phone. Ken was her late father, who had passed through to the higher life a few years previously. "You will get good grades," he said.

The sobs on the other end of the phone turned to gentle laughter. "He always believed in me, thought I would do well," she said as her voice began to choke a little with more emotion flowing through her.

Ken went on to describe the house they had lived in and sent his love to her mother, his much-adored wife. He continued by telling me to say he was aware his wife was about to move north from San Francisco with their son so she could be near their daughter in Washington while she completed her college studies.

"That's right. We're all going to live together again. It'll be great!" she exclaimed.

Judging by the smile I could see on Ken's face, he thought it was a good idea, too. "Your mom will be much happier now," he added.

As our session concluded the young woman enquired if her mother could contact me later on, as she had found the whole experience "life-changing" and felt her mother would wish to speak to me when she heard what had occurred in her daughter's session. I agreed and some weeks later the appointment was arranged.

Before I answered the telephone for her mother's call, Ken appeared to me, this time wearing his military uniform, complete with a splendid array of campaign and service medals that had been awarded to him over the years.

"Your husband is here already," I told her as I wished her good afternoon, only to be corrected by Ken who reminded me it was actually early morning where his wife was speaking from.

"He was very particular about time and punctuality," she said, her voice quivering slightly. "He liked to be early for everything."

Ken had died while still a serving officer. He proudly pointed to one of the medals he was wearing which I tried to describe to my caller. He then pretended he was going to pin the medal on her chest. She began to cry as I told her what he was doing.

"I went to receive that medal for him," she continued. "It was awarded to him after he had died."

I told her Ken then fired up a barbecue, cooking steaks and burgers, clearly in his element.

"He loved doing a barbecue. Any chance, even in bad weather, and he would get out the steaks and cook away."

There was happiness creeping through her sadness as she recalled these moments. Little things, but as we soon discover when those we love are no longer with us, little things really do mean a lot.

And then some ice cream appeared. There was some for him and some for her—the Baskin Robbins brand. "Pralines and Cream," Ken said with enthusiasm. His wife began to cry a little on her end of the phone so I paused for a moment before adding that there was "Rocky Road too!"

"That was his favourite," she exclaimed, her voice considerably warming. "And mine was Pralines and Cream."

She was quite astonished to hear this simple yet, for her, poignant message from her angel and eventually she began to chuckle and laugh. "He never forgot the ice cream. Never."

Our conversation continued as Ken recounted other stories.

Finally our visitor said, "The move will be good. It will work out just fine. Wish I could help you pack up. I love you—love you all," and then he was gone and I could see him no more.

But I am sure he would be back to look over his family from time to time—a warm, loving man when on the earth amongst his loved ones, now radiating that quality so powerfully from his new world.

CHAPTER 8

Angels of Mirth and Lighter Moments

*I*was generally a happy child. I loved to hear people laugh and still do. I vividly recall a situation from my school days when our teacher, Mr Jefferies, asked us what we wanted to be when we grew up. I was around 10 years old at the time and rather cheeky. There were the usual, expected replies—teacher, nurse, pilot, and so on—but my response was met with some disapproval, judging by the expression I can still recall on Mr Jefferies' face.

I announced my response with glee: "A comedian!" Judging by my school reports at the time, I did my best to put that into practice, frequently reducing my classmates to rounds of uncontrollable laughter before having my backside firmly warmed by the hand of my long-suffering teacher. In adult life I did work briefly in stand-up comedy, and mostly got it out of my system, although some of my clients and students today might argue otherwise.

The psychological benefits of laughter are of course now well researched and recognised, and beings from what we term the spiritual realms understand that too. They don't want to see us cry; they want to laugh and celebrate life, wherever it is, and they want us to join in that celebration with them.

Many years ago, early in my professional practice, a famous medium told me how we don't appear to lose our sense of humour when we step through into our next life. I must say

I was particularly pleased to hear so early on in my work as a clairvoyant, that I had by no means left humour behind. I knew from watching him demonstrate his fine mediumship and working with him many times that some of the angels seemed to deliberately bring humour or a lightness of touch in their communications, raising a smile or two to what is often an emotionally charged experience.

The communications mentioned here brought smiles and laughter to their recipients. To the casual observer, not the rip-roaring humour of a comedy show that would make us fall about with laughter, but they demonstrate the importance of those idiosyncratic events in family life and human behaviour that later take on a deeper significance for us that we so wish we could share again with those who have passed on. Even mildly irritating habits may become a topic for laughter when recalled by a visiting angel; precious memories of Grandad falling asleep, snoring loudly in his armchair only to awaken and complain that his tea was cold, or a silly catch-phrase our partner used in a tense or embarrassing moment. These are what I call "happy-sad moments" reminding us that although we miss our loved ones, we also cherish them and the little personal jokes we shared. I am pleased to have experienced this in my work.

Her father

The gentleman angel had given me no name or particular identification. It is not unusual to be given few, if any, clues as to whom the angels may be when they first appear. In fact, it is easy on occasion to confuse the information given because there may be a crossed wire in the spiritual circuitry when the contact attempting to be made is coming from two or more sources simultaneously, causing the spiritual switchboard to become temporarily jammed. Initially, in the case of this client's angel, I thought this was happening, as there seemed to be two streams of images and thoughts coming through to me.

Eventually things settled down and the father of Iris, the Swiss woman I was sitting with, gradually appeared until I could see him quite clearly. The confusion I experienced earlier lifted away. Iris was the mother of a friend, and I was with her in the new flat she had recently moved to in Zurich, where she was making a new home with her partner Ted.

Unemptied boxes were lined up around the place. Ted was still in North Carolina as he had matters to attend to at his former home. The permanent settling in Switzerland was an enormous change for a man approaching his retirement, but he and Iris had been a couple for some time and they both looked forward to their new life together in Zurich.

"He is showing me the work he used to do," I told Iris. Her father had been a highly skilled leather worker and saddle-maker, and he showed me not only the work he used to do when he was here on earth but also some of the tools he used.

Iris recognised the details in everything he showed to me as the memories flooded back to her from her childhood. He, in turn, offered words of encouragement as she embarked upon her new life. "Ted is a good man. He will be good for you," came his message. This helped Iris considerably. Although she loved Ted and had known him for years while he was working in Switzerland, she still experienced trepidation over the many changes taking place in her life.

Then a female angel, who had been Iris' mother-in-law from her earlier marriage, paid us a visit. She had loved to sew and had been very fond of Iris, recalling how she had taught Iris embroidery years ago. It is always interesting how simple memories of everyday moments can lift the spirits of those who are touched and reminded of them by loved ones from another world. They warm the heart and often stir tears of fond remembrance. Our visitor described a photograph in a box that had yet to be unpacked.

"I wasn't the prettiest," our angel remarked. "Wouldn't want my photo to spoil the décor of your nice new flat, now would you?"

It was a loving, humorous moment, and Iris chuckled, saying that the unpacking was just another big job yet to be done and assured her that she would love to have her picture out in view for all to see. She wasn't deliberately hiding her.

As our time was drawing to a close, Iris' father came forward again.

"And for goodness sake, let Ted hang those pictures on to the wall. They are valuable and need to be secure," our angel said with a broad smile creeping across his face, filling the entire room with its warmth as smiles can often do.

Suddenly, there was a loud crash in the hallway. Iris jumped up quickly and went to investigate, with me following behind.

There on the floor was a large painting that Iris had tentatively hung on the wall. She thought it would make the place look and feel more like home before Ted got back from the USA. She had made a valiant but ineffective effort to hang it and the heavy painting had crashed onto the carpet. The frame was a little damaged but the rest still intact, much to Iris's relief.

"Thank goodness!" she exclaimed, tears of laughter flowing down her face. "I'm so relieved. That one was my father's. He was a bit late warning me!"

A tooth problem

I talked to a young nurse whose grandmother had been like a mother to her. She adored her and her granny seemed very keen to make contact. Her granny appeared, showing many jars of homemade jam, marmalade and sundry pickles. Her grandmother had brought her up and there was a very strong bond between them. They had often cooked together, and this great homemaker of an angel had involved her granddaughter in all manner of baking and jam-making activities. Those times of informal, everyday activity in the kitchen were tender memories like those that so many of us carry deep in the recesses of our minds, waiting to surface in happy-sad moments of reflection and reverie.

Our communicating angel next held up a bird in her hands but I wasn't sure what variety it was.

"Helen Bird, her name was Helen Bird!" the excited young lady shouted.

The bird then changed into what I recognised as a swallow, and flew around a bright golden sun.

"And she lived in Swallow Close. She always used to joke that one swallow doesn't make a summer!"

Visiting angels often use symbols. There are many reasons for this, a primary one being that our subconscious minds communicate with us through symbols and pictures, the natural vocabulary of our imagination, our mind's visual picturing mechanism.

Then Granny placed a cricket bat into an empty glass jar, which I found puzzling, but my client knew immediately what the message was. As a child she had caught a grasshopper in a jar whilst playing in her granny's garden. She explained, "Granny said to me, 'Now you've got cricket in a jar.'"

It was a happy session, bringing much joy to this young nurse, who worked in our local hospital. Not all sessions flow so well. Some can be very difficult, the connection being not so easy to establish or maintain with these other worlds; or perhaps the information given is not recognised by the client, at least at that moment.

Then I told her that her granny was holding up some false teeth and they were dangling from a piece of string or cotton. Amidst the ensuing laughter, the nurse said that her grandmother had a great sense of humour and had often joked about her grandfather's false teeth, which he used to remove and place in a jar of cleaning liquid overnight.

"But these are broken," I told her.

I could see Granny comically dangling them before my eyes, and that the owner of those teeth was her grandfather, who was still alive.

"She says he has a problem with his teeth—that he is even more careless these days. Needs his teeth tied to his head she is telling me."

The nurse responded that she had spoken to him by phone that morning and that he would have said if there was a problem. She said she was sure his teeth were fine because when he forgets to put them in, he sounds like he is eating mushy peas as he speaks.

The session ended and the young lady left, happy that she had been in touch again with someone she loved so much, and who had a devilish sense of fun as well as fond memories. Later that day the nurse went to visit her granddad in the retirement home, as she often did.

Upon her arrival, she later told me, she was greeted by one of the staff wearing a slightly worried look on her face. "We've had just a little problem with your grandfather. It's his false teeth," she said. "He put them on a chair in his room, forgot about them and then sat on them, somehow breaking one set of teeth in half. To make matters worse he tried to fix them with a bit of fine string!"

It was just as her granny had showed me.

Enjoyed my funeral

I had helped Martin during his last illness. He had been to see me for healing with his wife, Angela, but despite his best efforts with healing, meditation, and various other therapies, Martin eventually passed into the higher life in 2003. A healer learns, as I had done over many years, that sometimes the physical curing of a patient's illness may not occur. Some could see this as failure, but it is not so, no matter how much physical wellness is desired. In such cases the healer accompanies the patient as they approach their journey into the next life, helping them to be better prepared and more able to let go in a peaceful state of mind.

Both Martin and Angela were open spiritually, having investigated many areas of religion and spiritual practice, including mediumship and psychic matters. Angela wrote a play, and also a book, *Only a Thought Away*, which explores life after death. It includes several accounts of angel contact including her visits to me both before and after Martin's death. So, Martin was at least partly prepared for some kind of continuing life after passing and believed that his spirit or identity would continue after death.

A few weeks after his funeral, Angela came to see me again. I remember the dark, cold January morning, the rain falling in buckets on the grey, bleak Suffolk countryside. Angela wanted a chat, maybe some closure on things and was hoping Martin would appear to spend some time with us.

For those who condemn psychics and mediums for summoning up the dead and disturbing their rest, let me say here that those who have moved on to higher lives or other worlds will only contact us if they wish to and are able to do so. No medium can guarantee who, if anyone, will communicate with us. We cannot summon them up at will, as they come out of love and not coercion. And, as I discuss in a later chapter, we certainly don't seem to rest in the next world despite the R.I.P. we often place on gravestones. As one wag put it—does it mean "Rest in Peace" or "Rise if Possible"? Well it's been my experience that we certainly don't rest on some celestial couch!

Martin did appear. He communicated on many issues; his love of his garden, the diary he had kept of his fight with cancer, his hobby of pottery and his experimentation with the various glazes he had developed. He also communicated to Angela some personal messages. There were his many books and he mentioned Saling, the village in which they had lived when he died. Martin and Angela had first met at the seafront of Aberystwyth and had sat together watching the sails of a small yacht as the sun went down. Subsequently they had agreed that whoever died first they would use the word "Saling" or "sailing" as a test word in any later after-life communication with a medium. I knew of course where they lived but was unaware of the other significance of the word "sailing" until he showed to me the beautiful image of sailing and the yachts where their relationship had begun and where they made their pact to return and mention "sailing" to the one left behind.

He mentioned "D" or Dee as she was called, asking me to thank her for tending to his feet. Angela enlightened me that Dee used to give Martin reflexology treatments when he was ill. He went on to refer to Angela's interest in the stage and a play of some kind, an interest that I had been unaware of.

"Are you in a play?" I asked her.

"I'm directing one."

"I ask you this because Martin is holding up a skull and reciting from Shakespeare's Hamlet, 'Alas, poor Yorik,' in a comical style like some ham actor!"

By this time Martin's dry sense of humour had begun to fill the room. Any sensitive individual would have felt it. So evident when he was alive, his wit had clearly not deserted him in his higher life.

Angela's jaw dropped in surprise. "I've got that book! On the kitchen table!" she exclaimed. "I read a lot about the theatre and about the 88 productions of Hamlet someone had seen. And the picture on the cover is someone holding the skull!" She was very excited and animated by now, and I could see that Martin was in full flow portraying the stereotypical amateurish thespian, overacting to his heart's content.

"He's obviously aware of that," I replied.

Angela and I both laughed at Martin's antics but he wasn't finished. When you are on a roll, you are on a roll, as we say, whatever world you inhabit it seems.

"Was there a beer at his funeral? He says he liked the beer." He had shown me a coffin on a hearse and a glass of beer. "He was pleased there was a beer," I continued.

"Well," a puzzled Angela answered, "we did have a bit of a 'knees-up' afterwards but nothing too much." She seemed unimpressed by this apparently trivial comment. However

Martin's humour had been at work. A few days later, a friend of Angela's who was reading through the transcript of our meeting, suddenly got it. "Not a beer—he meant BIER!" He had been given a "green" or "environmentally friendly" funeral as he had requested, including the traditional cart or hearse or bier as it is correctly known. His play on words and humorous symbolism had us all temporarily bemused.

Of course he had seen his funeral—those that have passed through often do. On many occasions I have watched grieving relatives, bowed in tearful sorrow during a funeral, with a visiting angel close by, trying to comfort them, listening to their own life being eulogised and celebrated. They will often view the flowers given in their memory and, on one occasion, I could see the dead man comically trying to conduct the badly sung hymns at his own funeral from the front of the church, saying "Sing up you lot, is that all you think of me?"

Sadly no one but me seemed to see him and the dirge continued. Martin had had his joke with us, too!

A comedian calls

This next tale concerns Sylvia. She came to see me in January 2008. Her husband Jim had passed over just six weeks earlier, having suffered a slow physical decline from Parkinson's disease. Sometimes our angels visit us relatively quickly after passing, within weeks or even days. The reasons for this are many, which I've found to be dependent upon the amount and nature of the adjustment time needed when we pass through and encounter a new state of being. This is particularly significant for those who experienced a traumatic death, those who really didn't want to die, or who held no intellectual concept or belief in any sort of continuing afterlife existence. I will discuss this in more detail in Chapter 9.

Jim was ready after a few weeks. However, Sylvia was concerned that Jim had suffered from medical negligence during the latter part of his illness as serious complications in his condition set in. She was in the process of lodging a formal complaint to the health authorities, not out of malice but because she wished the situation not to occur again so that Jim's suffering would not have been in vain. Jim appeared and immediately the atmosphere lightened. He had been a jovial man by nature, and the first thing he showed us was his love of the game bowls. Many will know this old game. Played on a flat green surface, usually of grass, the players roll large round, wooden bowls towards a smaller jack ball, the bowl nearest to the jack at the end of each game wins.

"What's a bias—he's mentioning bias?" I asked. The bias, Sylvia explained, is the piece of metal in the wooden bowl, or "wood" as they are known to the initiated, that encourages the curving motion, or bias, as the wooden bowl is rolled across the green by the player. I was unaware of this term and a three-way conversation got underway as both Jim and Sylvia enlightened me.

Jim told her that he missed her but that "her ticket (to where he now was) was not printed yet." He then started to sing an old 1940s comic song "Hang on the Bell, Nelly." He had been a bus conductor in his early life and was referring to this period when London conductors would press a bell to tell the driver it was safe to move away, often calling out for the benefit of any standing passengers, "Hang on now please!" In those days conductors also issued brightly coloured tickets to passengers as they paid their fares.

Other angels then joined us, including Sylvia's aunt Cath, who had been very close to her. She reminded Sylvia of the

Bible she possessed with her aunt's name written in it, and she also mentioned the fine china, which she left to Sylvia in her will, and some special advice on health and nutrition she felt Sylvia should note. This was apparently typical of her aunt. One day Aunt Cath presented us with a raw salad, suggesting it was food we should eat more often. Cath had been a vegetarian cook, lecturing on nutrition and vegetarianism in the 1940s—a woman ahead of her times in many ways.

Sylvia paid me several return visits and each time she received what she described as accurate evidence from her family and, of course, Jim.

He spoke of his awareness of the twists and turns in the legal investigation into his diagnosis and treatment, explaining that he was now free from pain and suffering but that it had been necessary. "It was karma, not punishment; something from another lifetime."

This was just one of many references made by angel communicators to the idea that we somehow experience many lifetimes or incarnations on this planet and many situations we encounter in one life are the consequences of an earlier one in another time. Karma simply means cause and effect, the biblical reaping and sowing.

But then the mood lightened once more and Jim the comedian made his presence felt. I didn't know, prior to Jim's visits, that as a young man he had tried his luck as an entertainer, a comedian and actor. As so many of us do, he concluded that success in such work would elude him, so he pursued other jobs and careers. But once a comedian always a comedian, and Jim proved to be no exception. Even his descriptions of painful memories were laced with humour. He sang to me, "I wish I could shimmy like my sister Kate. She shimmies like a jelly on a plate," words of a song he had sung to Sylvia as she gave him the jelly and ice cream he often had to be fed as his illness took hold and he experienced difficulty in swallowing.

He entertained Sylvia and me several times. "Each time I listen to the recording (of the sessions) it's impossible not to join in with the laughter," she told me. "There is such a strong empathy between Jim and you. You had both been Redcoat entertainers at the famous Butlins Holiday camps in your younger years, paid to entertain and make people laugh."

Jim went on to speak about many things, like the children's story character, "Thomas the Tank Engine," and stood before us attired in an old-fashioned train driver's hat. He had always wanted to experience that dream of so many young boys of his generation—driving a steam engine.

He sang other funny songs, which carried so much significance for her, evoking thoughts of many happy memories of their life together. Jim encouraged her to cook his favourite rice puddings, to play her piano again. "Come on Sparky!" he chided, a reference to the story of Sparky and his Magic Piano.

But he saved the best laugh for Sylvia until his last contact. He put on a lady's wig, and showed me a television advertisement for L'Oréal hair care products. "I am worth it!" he said to me in a mock French accent. Sylvia almost fell off her chair with astonishment, by now crying with laughter at this other world cabaret that her Jim was providing for her. I didn't get the joke. "That is so amazing!" she cried out. "Towards the end of his life, Jim used to be very amused by these words from the slightly self-mocking L'Oréal advert and often said to me and his care-givers, 'Because I am worth it!' as we sometimes struggled to help him move and eat his meals. It was his way of laughing at himself and his difficult situation."

A true angel of mirth was our Jim: one who succeeded in making the wife who missed him so much laugh until she ached as he recalled lighter moments he shared with her during his final illness. It was a most healing experience.

"Where's yer troosers!"

One morning whilst I waited in my office for my first client of the day to arrive, I became aware of a comically dressed angel who also seemed to be waiting for someone. He was wearing a Scottish tartan kilt, many sizes too big for him, which hung to just above his ankles. On his feet were a large pair of black boots, and above his waist he sported a floppy old-fashioned string vest. To crown it all, upon his head was an enormous Tam o' Shanter hat complete with huge bobble, almost covering his ears. He had a narrow, thin face and a little moustache. His presence could perhaps best be described as cheeky, a character not too concerned with others' opinions of him. There was no message coming from him, so I assumed that he had appeared a little prematurely to contact my first visitor.

This sometimes happens, as angels, not surprisingly, seem to know in advance of such meetings and are often far better prepared for the occasion than we are. Limits of time and space as we know them are not the restrictions for them that they are for us.

When my first client settled in the chair opposite to me, I asked her if she recognized this man as I described him to her. She didn't know him at all. Since he seemed to make no attempt to communicate with her, I ignored him while I got on with the needs of the client.

My first session done, I sat back in my chair and asked him who he was. But he simply grinned and said nothing. I also drew a blank with the next client.

"I haven't got a clue who he is," was the response, and our amusingly clad visitor seemed content just to stand and watch. So I again cleared him from my mind and continued working. I was a bit puzzled, I must confess, because it is rare that our angels get the timing wrong when a friend or family member visits a clairvoyant.

My final client of the morning arrived and immediately I could hear the unmistakable droning sound of Scottish bagpipes that one seems to either love or hate. The music, if I dare to call it that for it wasn't particularly competent playing, echoed from around our patiently waiting visitor. Then he burst into song, prancing around as he did so, filling the ethers with the sound of "Donald, Where's Yer Troosers?" the comic Scottish song made famous by the singer and entertainer Andy Stewart. I described what I could see and hear to the lady sitting near me.

"Och, that's my dad," she said, a beautiful smile spreading across her bright face. "He always dressed in that silly way for Hogmanay, The New Year. He was called Donald, so he would sing it to us after he'd had a few drinks and lost his inhibitions, clowning away and making us all laugh."

There was no mistaking this angel's dress and performance for anyone else—a loving dad performing once more to make his beloved daughter smile.

CHAPTER 9

What do You do in Heaven?

~⚬~

*P*laying a harp or sitting on a cloud in a cherubic pose has never held much appeal for me. Thankfully, my work has clearly shown me that whatever "Heaven" may be for us, sitting on a cloud is not it. There is a continuation of a purposeful life after what we term death and what we actually do in the next life has long intrigued me, just as it has occupied the thoughts of many, including, no doubt, those reading this book.

I have had many out-of-the-body experiences, the state where our personal consciousness or self-awareness leaves the physical body and appears to lift upwards unhindered by the constraints of the physical world. My first experience in this state was when I was struck by lightning as a teenager. On that occasion I became aware that the real "me" was not my unconscious and slightly barbecued physical body, lying on the floor of the tent. From my new viewpoint, the tent became so transparent it was almost invisible. The real me, Paul, had suddenly become the observer.

It was a little like looking at a relative or friend I know well, but not me. I was not aware of being located anywhere in particular at the time. I just wasn't on the earth anymore until my great grandma appeared and told me to "Go back." In that moment, I rapidly moved from a warm, almost blissful state, to find myself waking up burned, in pain, partially paralysed, and with the stench of scorched flesh in my nostrils. It was a remarkably invigorating and liberating experience to be out of my body, free from pain, just happy, with a very peaceful sensation filling the space around me.

Throughout my life I often consciously leave my body as I go to sleep. I become aware of other levels or states of being, observing "Paul" asleep on the pillow as I float upwards, pulled by some compelling force encouraging me to get away from here for a while. (One brief dividend of this is that I always look younger at that moment, about 25, however when I awake in the morning the ravages of time always reappear, wrinkles and all.) I also have a pre-birth memory, still extremely vivid, of the moments before I entered this life.

In my work I have been honoured to have communication with those who can begin to answer the question of what we do in heaven. I have come to know there is not just one reality but other tangible, conscious realities beyond this earth. Experiences later in my life, a few of which are mentioned in this book, confirm that. So, re-incarnation apart, what do we do when we have left here and we are no longer living in this earthly, physical way? As one student asked, "What do we do between lives?"

The following pages relate some exchanges with angels who sought to enlighten me as to what activities they pursue, what life is like for them, who they meet and so on.

In this state, there appears to be no disease, at least in the physical and mental ways we endure it on earth, no shortage of food or famine, and no need for money. Sounds like heaven to me; or paradise. Take your pick.

One angel who came forward to educate me was an old friend in this life who died comparatively young. He visits me often from his new world, and has tried on a few occasions to explain a little of what he does and what he found upon what we call "death," or rather transition to another world.

He and I originally became close pals after his wife organised some courses for me to teach near their home. Not especially enamoured with some of the spiritual people he had met, he initially viewed me with polite caution, as just another "New Ager." However we went on to become great friends, and it was a privilege to be told by him that I was the person who largely changed his view and attitude toward psychic and spiritual matters. Over time he attended many of my courses and had private sessions with me, unfolding a friendship, which I was surprised to learn, continued after he died.

"When I got here it was like waking up after sleep. I was still me, but lighter, not so heavy," he reported soon after he passed on.

"Do you have a body?" I asked.

"Yes mate, that's what you are looking at now." I could see him distinctly in this contact and he looked just as I remembered him before he became ill and passed on. He had developed a way of announcing himself to me that I would recognise instantly. Seated on a settee like the one he had in his home on earth where I used to visit him, he would raise a glass either of gin and tonic, or malt whisky, informing me that the "bar is open." This alluded to the fact that he and his wife had a rule that alcoholic drinks were never served before six p.m. on weekdays, though he and I stretched that rule on many occasions.

Like me, he was named Paul, and when he first appeared to me a year or so after his passing, he gave me evidences of who he was by discussing our motor bike rides together and reminding me of some of the ridiculous jokes we shared.

He asked me, "Are you Whistler's mother?" a reference to a comment he once made as we walked home from the pub one night in pouring rain. The flimsy white hood of my anorak was flapping around my head like a huge wet handkerchief buffeted by the strong wind, largely obscuring my face as we tried to chat. His contact was always laced with the unmistakeable dry sense of humour he possessed when alive. I think Whistler's mother, seated in her quiet pose for her famous portrait, may not have been amused, but I was. In his contact as an angel, he went on to try to explain in simple terms what he now did.

It appears that Paul, who was originally trained as an engineer, was involved in something similar in his new reality. But, perhaps the most thought-provoking idea was his next statement. "It is quite easy here to be in more than one place at what appears to be the same time."

This is an idea much suggested by researchers into the afterlife and the reader may like to review the findings of The Veritas Program at the University of Arizona, directed by Dr. Gary Schwartz, which supports this theory, and Paul's information.

"Time, the way you experience it, doesn't really exist here. I can multi-task," Paul told me.

"I'd find that very useful," I replied. I could hear his laughter.

Paul always thought I was a little disorganised, so more than one task at a time would have been beyond me it seemed to him, in whatever dimension I found myself.

I asked him, "What do you do in that world? Is it like a holiday, as you can obviously do many things there?"

He explained that he was now also a kind of engineer but with what we would call "light," or a type of super electricity. Paul was particularly intrigued by the way different frequencies of light and energy interacted and how some human beings, like me, had found a way of being consciously more aware of other higher frequencies and fields of light, and were able not only to view them but interact with them at will.

"That's why I came to visit you. To watch when you are working and to understand how what you do functions. Sometimes, I and some other beings here help the process." There was a pause and then, "And because I truly loved you as a friend and wanted to help you." For a man who sometimes hid his true feelings, this was a deeply poignant statement. We had lots of fun together, much laughter, and I do miss his physical presence.

"I watch what is going on as a conscious contact is made from dimension to dimension, frequency to frequency. I watch people like you and do what I can to help sometimes, a bit like helping with the invisible wiring and circuits. It is like electricity."

I found this particularly interesting. Most psychics, me included, often have unusual effects upon the electrical equipment around them, indicating that there is an invisible current of some kind involved. I have blown up vacuum cleaners, stopped electric clocks and even managed to turn the TV on and off a few times without any contact with switches— long before the emergence of remote control devices. There was a long-standing family joke that I should never be allowed near electrical equipment; it was years before I could use a computer without it going haywire. Fortunately, I learned to control this phenomenon. Furthermore, so called "hauntings," as I mentioned in Chapter 3, are commonly linked to unusual electrical activity that appears to have no obvious, logical material cause.

"Do you remember you and the optician?" He laughed as he referred to this particular incident. "I was watching you then." It occurred some years ago, when during an eye test, I was asked by the optometrist if I used a computer.

"No, I don't," I told her. "I have an adverse effect on electrical things, so I leave them alone."

I remember her disbelieving frown as my words obviously went against her more scientific sensibilities. Shortly afterwards, her face contorted in disbelief and frustration as she struggled to adjust the machine that does the "puff" pressure test on the eyeball when it simply broke down and refused to function. After wrestling unsuccessfully with the machine she left the consulting room, seeking a replacement while muttering, "It was working okay with the last patient."

I confess to a wry smile creeping across my face. However, I quickly did some deep breathing, which I had earlier discovered seemed to be a remedy for my unwanted electrical problems. I didn't want to sit there all day.

"She wound you up a bit, mate, and the effect was that you blew the thing as the power surged in you. It's that amongst other things I am interested in and work with."

He went on to say that much of what he does, as he evolves and understands more of how his own mind and energies work, is difficult to describe.

"It can sound a bit like science fiction," he said. "I can watch thoughts and thought fields pulse and move and know how to improve and influence them constructively—but you can do that. It's simply much clearer here, as there is proportionately less dense matter than in your dimension."

Over several contacts Paul attempted to describe to me how in this higher and seemingly parallel dimension there was still what we would describe as matter, but the proportion of dense matter to energy and light was very different. He explained there is much less matter so everything is easier to change. Therefore, controlling thought consciously is the mechanism by which they function. We are less adept at that here in this world and circumstances change more slowly as a consequence.

"The impact of your thought is much more immediate here, and more accurate. So you have to control your mental processes more carefully. It takes a bit of getting used to but after some practice and education it makes life very interesting and more efficient." Paul said.

"It's the same for you where you are, but slower, and requires persistence. What you call negative thinking, doubt, and worry all block manifestation, especially of the things you desire. But, anything is possible on earth if you are constructive, positive, and don't give up. It is based on electrical particles and magnetism, but you weren't much good at science at school, were you?"

Paul was right about my casual approach to science. As a young boy, I found it puzzling, due to the abstract manner in which it was taught to me. But I found this information from Paul enthralling. As I looked back at my many achievements in this lifetime, I was very surprised to discover that the ideas I didn't give up on eventually came about, often in unexpected and thrilling ways.

I have had many more conversations with Paul; most are not concerning the afterlife. They are more about guidance and the understanding of earthly issues in the here and now. But the glimpses he was able to share of the afterlife I found most heartening and fascinating.

Helping people transition in death

From time to time, a visiting angel may refer briefly to an activity in which they are involved in their new life. A common one is helping souls who are leaving or about to leave this world, often lovingly aiding members of their own family as they make their transition. This caring service given to us by our angels illustrates for me that, however difficult and painful things may appear to be for us on the earth sometimes, the true nature of our cosmos is one of love, compassion, and support for all life, whatever form it takes. It is by no means just a continuation of what we have here.

I have often accompanied someone in the last moments of their earthly life, sometimes hearing them describe the presence of long-dead loved ones around them, as my own mother did. Her sister and brother became visible to both her and me at the foot of her bed. As the physical sheath we call our body fades and weakens we do begin to see more clearly the higher dimensions that await us.

On other occasions the angels spend a period assisting other souls who find the immediate post-death moments difficult, even believing for a while that they are still alive. This can be the case particularly for those who have no belief in life after death or have led an unpleasant and nasty life, being selfish and excessively materialistic.

Another common theme expressed by angels is that we are here mainly to serve others and to explore and unfold God's love in us and through us. And for a while after passing on, we may seek to help those still living on the planet who, in turn, seek to help humanity one way or another to create a better world. My experience suggests there is no hell or purgatory except that of our own making. Some souls who have led unpleasant, nasty lives will have to examine their behaviour in the next world after their death, so that they may learn from their actions and awaken more fully, allowing the beautiful light in them to shine brightly once more.

In the previous chapter I told the story of Martin and his contact with his widow after his passing. Martin had more to add to this conversation, reporting that despite what we believe, most people in the Western world still see this life as a complete, one-time-only experience, believing there is no re-incarnation, and little possibility of activity beyond death. He implied that while we in the room believed in the continuation of life and were enthusiastic to learn more about how he was able to be highly creative with both elements of his mind—the logical scientist and the creative artist—others would not share our view of what was happening to him, nor would they share our interest.

As he developed his pottery in the latter part of his life, he deeply wished to do something even more creative, more beautiful. So Life said, *Okay, step through. This is the chance.* By "stepping through" into that expanded, greater state of being experienced in the next world, he was now able to accomplish even more wonderful things.

Martin explained a little of what happened to him immediately after his passing. He found himself in a room of some kind. "You are given an environment in which you feel comfortable," he had told me. He was taken through things to reach an understanding of what had happened, by some other beings who had helped him with this process. This may be a reference to the kind of "life review" others have mentioned where we look at how we did in this life to learn from our experiences. Not so much a judgement but a chance for each of us to have a look and see how we have done while here.

"Everything is done to make you feel stable. I looked about 40 years old!"

Martin then showed me what appeared to be a piece of paper, which was actually a map of some kind. For different people it is shown in different ways, but for him it was a map of where he'd come from, and why things had been the way they were.

"It was like a diagram of explanation that suited my mind," he said.

His wife smiled when I told her. When he was alive here and working in his profession as a planner, she confirmed he always felt at home somewhere once he had a map. What an appropriate way to help Martin re-orientate to his new world!

He met what he described as a "being," a woman called Marianna. This person was like a teacher who gathered together certain souls to prepare them for what was going to come next. He then had a choice, he was told. He was offered something like a holiday in his astral nature, where he could do anything he wished to, and have anything he wanted. (The astral world is the part of the higher planes closest to earth, where we find ourselves just after death.)

What Martin told us concurred with Paul's revelations, in that we can make anything we think of manifest much more easily in the next dimension—with some possibility of easy wish fulfilment until the need or desire is expiated and when we then feel ready to get on with something else more purposeful. Or we get straight on with a task, which is part of our growth in that new dimension, which is what Martin did. This did not surprise his wife, as Martin always had wanted to get on with things. It was typical of him, she told me.

The next piece of information was especially interesting. Martin's wife said it literally took her breath away. Martin told me that part of his new work involved "the spirits of the minerals." This was particularly significant because as part of his university degree course Martin studied geology. I was unaware of this, and his wife went on to tell me that he loved stones, rocks and fossils, and that years ago he had often taken part in field trips, complete with his geological hammer. Furthermore, his wife informed me, he was especially interested in minerals in the last years of his life, experimenting with them in the various glazes he made for his pottery.

Martin told me, "It's difficult to put into words. If you can think that all the minerals have spirits, my job is to help these spirits as the earth changes." He continued, "I'm helping the consciousness of the planet. That's my main job at the moment."

But he was also doing something else. He explained, as Paul did earlier, that he could be in more than one place at a time. He was also involved in prayer and temple construction—not the physical ones as we would imagine, but energy spaces, which are temple-like in design, linked to the thoughts of prayer in some way. This made sense to his wife because Martin had not only had a professional involvement with buildings and environments on earth, as a Quaker he had also been a man of prayer and spiritual practice.

He showed me some symbols in an attempt to explain matters further, but I failed to ascertain their meaning despite Martin's and my subsequent best efforts. However, the information he shared with us was more than sufficient to confirm that we certainly keep busy after death. And for a man who always liked to be useful, Martin's new reality gave him plenty of opportunity to be just that.

CHAPTER 10

Angels or Ghosts?

⁓⁓⁓

In this matter-of-fact material world, where nothing is believed until we can supposedly scientifically prove it, many of us still seem to hanker after the mysterious, the supernatural and illogical, even if it sends a chill down our spines when such stories tell of eerie visitations and wailing spectres floating around in the dead of night. After all, even if it isn't true, some of us find it exciting.

Still, there are the questions: Is what we see psychically an illusion? Is it some kind of collective memory or ghost, or really the spirit of some visiting angel whom we may or may not have known, who still exists, albeit in another world or reality of some kind? How can we know?

Spirits or angels?

In this chapter the stories illustrate the differences between what we may refer to as a ghost versus a visiting angel.

The town I live in is an old, but still growing, English market town called Bury St. Edmunds. With its rich history, it provides an excellent research laboratory for my work. There was a magnificent abbey here in the Middle Ages dedicated to the first English Christian martyr, St. Edmund, King of the East Angles, who was slain by the invading Danes. A prominent and prosperous monastery grew up around his shrine, inhabited by Benedictine monks and ruled by a succession of abbots. It

105

became an early place of pilgrimage, and the town is full of ghostly legends and stories, many involving those inevitable hooded monks of times gone by. It was also a favourite stopping off place for the author Charles Dickens, who spent much time here writing and giving readings in the Athenaeum building. Perhaps the many ghostly legends influenced his writing on the subject, for example, *A Christmas Carol*, which abounds with ghosts. He mentions the town in his well-known novel, *The Pickwick Papers*. There are tales of Dickens' ghost appearing in the Angel Hotel, where he stayed, especially in the Dickens Room.

Taking time amidst the abbey ruins of this town, a sensitive individual will feel the antiquity of the place. Though most people won't be aware of it, the energy and memories of what happened years before is still palpable, like a silently playing record or a film running quietly in the background. Anyone remotely psychically aware will have a field day walking around the town centre, visiting the abbey gardens and pausing in one of its various hotels, tearooms and restaurants. Bury St. Edmunds provides the sensitive a wonderful opportunity to experience the difference between ghosts and other types of spiritual visitors, as the following stories serve to illustrate.

One early evening I was having supper with two friends in a small restaurant in the town centre, located in a sloping street called Abbeygate Street, which passes downwards to Angel Hill, opposite the Abbey Gate. This gate was once the people's entrance to what was the Abbey's courtyard, and is now a public gardens. Most of the buildings in the town itself postdate the Abbey, since there was a large fire in Bury in the 1600s, shortly after the Great Fire of London, destroying most of the mediaeval properties.

As we enjoyed our meal, I noticed two black-robed figures appearing to emerge through a brick wall close to our table. Dressed as monks, they came over to where I sat. They looked to be in their twenties and seemed aware that I could not only feel, but also see them. Another of my companions also sensed something unusual, telling me that the hairs stood up on the back of her neck and the air had cooled around her. As I mentioned earlier, such temperature changes and the arousal of the nervous system are commonly experienced by those encountering the supernatural, as psychic energy is stimulated in us and briefly utilised in its manifestation, whether we are aware of it or not.

One of the monks was quite jolly, while the other was more sombre. They began to communicate with me as I informed my fellow diners of our invisible visitors. They explained that they had been lay brothers, not ordained priests, who performed some of the menial tasks around the Abbey during the 14th century. The quieter one had been called Thomas and had worked as a cook. He told me how he grew herbs for his cooking, especially in the preparation of meat for the Abbot's table. He also used to help with the brewing of beer, a usual monastic practice in those days. The River Lark, which flows next to the Abbey ruins, provided the necessary water suitable for brewing purposes. Thomas looked a bit miserable, unhappy in fact, so his more jovial companion, who gave no name, took over the conversation.

"Did you see us come through that wall?" he asked. "It wasn't there in our day. The buildings were different then, so this wall you now see didn't exist for us and still doesn't, although we are aware of it existing for you." He laughed as he said those words. His voice had a strange accent, which I didn't recognise but his English was being transmitted to me clearly. Obviously his everyday language of the time would have been largely indecipherable to me, so fortunately our communication was in words I could understand. Sometimes this can be a problem, especially when an angel uses a different language in its thought process and my mind can't readily convert it to English. In such situations, a translation usually begins and my mind locks into theirs, as happened in this case. The thoughts they transmit and "speak" are a universal language, just like in telepathic exchanges, whereas verbal language is local, evolving and changing over time. Any student of English literature who has read Milton and Chaucer can attest to that.

The happy monk explained there had been an apothecary where the restaurant site was now. He said the treatment room in the basement was visited by some of the monks for a variety of reasons, including help for sexually transmitted infections. The monks visiting for this reason would not want to be seen, since they were supposedly celibate.

He recounted that near the abbey wall, not far from the Norman Tower, was a brothel that some of the brethren would visit to enjoy female company. He smirked, looking at his glum companion, who, he went on to say, had caught something there, so he came to this place to fetch ointment for his sores.

No wonder Thomas looked depressed. As these words came to me, and before I had any opportunity to communicate them to my friends, one of them suddenly sat up with a start. Our jocular angel had placed a hand upon her thigh and she could feel a tingling sensation on her skin.

The monk smiled as I gently admonished him. "It was just a joke. I didn't mean to offend. Please say sorry to the lady."

"Apology accepted." I confirmed. I asked him why they were appearing to me in that moment, since their lives in this place went back centuries ago.

"It was an important life for us. We learned much and had a great affection for the place, and so a part of us returns to connect again with those memories and to look through at what is happening now in this time, your time."

This was a fascinating statement, suggesting that a part of his nature could visit Bury St. Edmunds in the 21st century but other parts of him did not—being in more than one place at the same time as other angels, mentioned in earlier accounts, have indicated to me is actually possible.

He continued, "And the linear time you experience now also doesn't exist once you are no longer physical. So we can be like time travellers, going backwards and forwards at will, once we have mastered it properly."

At this point I felt a change. It was clear that the monks were, like all of us, spirits who have had many lives and experiences of which the current life is but one. When we are no longer restricted by the physical body, we are not so limited in our functioning. I was no longer speaking to a cheeky monk who enjoyed embarrassing his friend, but an experienced soul who appeared to me, initially at least, in a form that I could recognise and had been his physical body when alive in this town hundreds of years ago. That part of him was like a costume he had worn in a scene from a play in which he had been a monk, and he was "wearing" it again for us. His words and insights transcended the intellectual range one would expect from a mediaeval lay brother. However, he soon took on his monk role again and his voice changed as he became a little less profound in his exchanges with me.

"We'll go now and leave you in peace. Come along, Thomas. Come on. Farewell, my friends, and may God bless you." And with that they vanished.

These two were true angels or messengers from another time, connecting with us not because we were relatives or friends who knew them in this earthly life, but because we had in common a geographic link in our love for a fine old town, albeit, enjoyed in different centuries.

Ghosts

With angels you may have a varied dialogue and be given information and ideas that no ghost could share with you. Angels, who are of the human family as we all are, are complete souls or spiritual beings. They, like us, are what I term "God in a Box" and have the entirety of God or the "Father" within them, even though much of it is dormant and not expressed or evident most of the time. Ghosts are different. They are not complete souls. They are residual energies or memories locked into the invisible energy field of a location, playing back like an old movie for those able to witness them. Angels exhibit neither the detached eeriness nor repetitive actions that soulless ghosts tend to evidence.

I often see visitors from other times—or at least their ghosts— walking, almost gliding along an old street as our monks did. They too disappear through walls, reappearing through one of the many old tunnels dug into the chalk under the old town.

Here in Bury St. Edmunds are ghosts aplenty, figures drifting around like a scene from another drama in time gone by. Unlike angels, they are oblivious to the observer, as they perform repetitive actions and scenarios, like puppets worked by some invisible puppet master over whom they have no influence. On return visits the psychic may well see the same ghostly characters, going through the same motions, time after time. Occasionally they will appear to look at you, but then you notice that they look through you as if you didn't exist. They may even seem to talk to you, but usually they rather talk "at" you, repeating the same thoughts. There is no conversation of merit, no real exchanges with a ghost.

They not only ignore the more recent buildings that have been constructed, as if unaware of them, but also may appear to float or be lacking feet, even lower portions of their legs or bodies, as they function on the land levels that existed in their time, often lower than today's surfaces and pathways.

In esoteric terms they are often called "astral shells," the astral world being the plane of feeling we pass through when we pass on. While we are on earth, every experience we have, indeed every thought and action, is imprinted in the invisible energy field of the planet. These experiences are like footprints, left in snow, permanent witnesses to events of the past. They are there whether we see them or not. Where the energy field of a locality is particularly dense or strong, these imprints are stronger too. This is especially true when events are or have been more highly emotionally charged, with either happiness or sadness, making these memories more powerful and therefore more accessible to those of us who feel or see them. Hence powerful high-energy sites become renowned as places of famous ghost sightings where many report similar experiences, seeing the same ghosts and apparitions. As more visitors flock to such places of spooky repute, our own emotional excitement adds to the energy of the spot, increasing the likelihood of seeing or feeling something, even if a figment of our own creative imagination. (One can be trained to know and interact consciously with the energy of people, animals, and places but that is not essentially the remit of this book: see my book, *Auras and Colours*.)

I remember sitting one night in the Fox Inn, one of the few buildings in the town that survived the fire in Bury in the 17th century. A male figure appeared wearing a tailcoat, breeches and riding boots. He sat on an invisible chair near the fire as his boots were pulled off by some other entity I couldn't see, and then hung on hooks near the fireplace. He looked around the room, not acknowledging anyone, then bent over, putting his head in his hands. Then he vanished, to reappear some twenty minutes later, repeating exactly the same actions as before. I saw this visitor four or five times that evening, each time going through the same motions, seemingly unaware of the roomful of us twentieth century occupants of the old building. That was a ghost.

When encountering any being or ghost we should always acknowledge it and give a blessing of some kind from our hearts. It is someone's memory, imprinted in the atmosphere from an earlier time, and we should respect it.

Trapped or earthbound souls

In the excellent film *Ghost*, the character played by the late Patrick Swayze dies, and at first doesn't realise his changed state. Once he does awaken to the fact he is no longer alive in his physical body he locates a medium, marvellously portrayed by Whoopi Goldberg. With the assistance of the professional medium he is able to contact the wife he left behind on earth. He then works to prevent his wife's murder before moving on to a heaven-like plane at the end of the movie. He wasn't a trapped soul, as some have mistakenly believed the story implies, but one of the truly earthbound entities or spirits so often described.

Those are souls who are temporarily trapped close to the consciousness of the earth either because they are slow in realising they have passed on to the higher life or because some emotionally charged experiences or memories from their earth life are still dominating their conscious minds. They continue to remain for a time after death within the limits of this material life, not yet aware of the greater world they now inhabit. Such beings may have died in a traumatic way and the shock of the experience lingers on, going round and round in their minds, until they awaken and move on to the more expansive and liberating existence that awaits them. This eventually happens as other angels help them "turn to the light," as it is termed, and guide them to understand their new reality with all its wonders.

Many of us have had the experience of waking up after a night's sleep, briefly unable to remember where we are. For some, arriving in the next life can be similar. If necessary, those beings are helped to become aware of where they are and who they are. In time, all angels realise this and adjust to their new life.

As I have mentioned, what is referred to as an earthbound soul or trapped spirit is often a ghost-like creature, a memory of some intensity that behaves just like a human being but, again, in true ghost fashion, goes through repetitive patterns of speech and action. You cannot have a meaningful and varied conversation with such entities as these.

There are some angels who may be called earthbound in one sense. Sometimes it may be that after death an individual's attachment to certain aspects of physical life lingers on in their minds and they yearn for it still, even though they can no longer have the same sensory connection. They remain drawn magnetically to memories, experiences, those they love, things they loved and even things they hated. They may be aware they are no longer here on the physical earth, but neither are they yet fully open to the beautiful higher frequencies. This state may be what has been termed "limbo" by some religions.

Those of us on earth can still help them through positive prayers of love and peace. Such invocations generate light on the higher planes and also aid those properly trained and experienced with mediumistic "rescue" work. This work directly helps bewildered angels who exist in a state akin to a partial sleep, or who repeatedly relive the memory of a traumatic death, to awaken more fully to the beautiful light that awaits them.

After the transition of death, we eventually find our way to our new existence, as it is the natural and inevitable way of things. Only a few souls—a truly small number—take longer to adjust, but adjust they always do.

Being prepared

It is good to prepare for death whilst we are still healthy and well. Our modern secular approach to life and death often produces a fear of this life ending, augmented by an accompanying lamentable ignorance of what may come next, or, worse still, a complete disbelief in the possibility that we continue to exist at all. Thus, death has become a taboo, not to be discussed in polite company until, that is, just before we have to face the fact that the inevitable passing from earth is going to happen to us and we hope to goodness the sceptics are wrong.

In Chapter 13, I suggest simple ways by which we may be more open to our own angel visitors and the blessings, comfort and love they seek to share with us.

CHAPTER 11

Your Angels

⌒☰⌒

Whether we know it or not, we are all visited frequently by unseen visitors or angels of many kinds. Some of these messengers are our loved ones or ancestors who have already passed through to the higher planes. I use the term "passed through" as that is what we seem to do—pass from this world to another more expansive one. Many visitors we knew well as our parents, partners, grandparents, aunts and uncles, or children. Others we may have known slightly or not at all. But they bring us their message of love and caring, revealing a deep interest in our progress here in this world, a world that they once experienced. They, too, knew the highs and lows of this earthly existence.

Guiding angels

There are those who may be termed "guiding angels." They were also human, but were not necessarily directly related to us. They come to us for a variety of reasons. Maybe they were our teachers in times gone by, or are what are often termed guides, interested in our development as spiritual beings, seeking to help us on our way as an invisible back-up team that, should we so desire, will have direct conscious contact with us where and when it is appropriate. These beings do not rule our lives, as some would have us believe, but guide and support us as we make decisions and choices. Most of us will never know them in any conventional sense. They are not with us to interfere or control, for that impinges on our freedom. But should we ask, with a sincere and open heart, they will help us to think with greater clarity so we may make our decisions in a more informed manner. Seeking to know our guides out of plain curiosity misses the point of their presence in our lives; they will not respond to trivial or ego-fueling requests.

My own guides, whom I have been aware of since childhood, do not interfere in my day-by-day life except when I face difficult problems. In such circumstances they will encourage me to think in the right way so solutions may emerge and the path forward becomes clearer. They certainly help, but it is I who has to take whatever action is necessary since this is my life and my chance to learn and grow. Their great value is in their directing me to develop and trust my own intuitive guidance in moments of doubt and difficulty. Their help is never imposed upon me but offered as a result of my request in keeping with a fundamental spiritual law—*ask and you will receive.*

We all have some freedom within the framework of our responsibilities and commitments for this life,. The more we unfold and evolve spiritually, the more that creative freedom becomes available, enabling us to experience greater inner direction or intuition, more consciously shaping our lives. To discover and unfold this beautiful power within us is the whole point in being here. Your own guides will never impose themselves upon you usurping that principle of choice, but they are there, waiting silently on the edge of your world, ready to assist you as you walk your path to your destiny.

There are also guides who are interested in some aspect of our work or vocation, sometimes becoming directly involved, as was the case with Chopin in an earlier story. My own work and research on the human aura has been very much assisted by the late C. W. Leadbeater, the famous Theosophist and clairvoyant. Those who practice the healing arts, for example, are undoubtedly part of a team with many invisible helpers working alongside them. Such angels as these are not earthbound, but as part of their task, have a commitment to support the many creative and healing endeavours taking place on the earth.

One of my clients, a surgeon, related how she is not only aware of her patient's relatives "looking through" but also other angels who assist her in the procedures she performs during an operation. She has also witnessed a patient's spiritual form rise up from the physical body, supported in some manner by the various angels around the operating table.

The celebrated healer George Chapman worked directly in his healing practice with Doctor William Lang, a former ophthalmic surgeon who had worked at the Middlesex Hospital in London. His story is most convincing and worth reading in the various books written about him, including *Healing Hands* by Bernard Hutton. Dr. Lang's children were so convinced that their father's angelic presence worked with George that they donated the late doctor's desk to him to use in his practice room.

Traditional angels

Among the many theories and classifications of angels that exist in Western Christianity, the one most commonly known is the Hierarchy of Dionysius, based upon the book *On the Celestial Hierarchy*. This work is attributed to an individual called Psuedo-Dionysius the Areopagate and it appeared around the fourth or fifth century. Within this order we find everything from the traditional guardian angels who are reputed to look after us individually, to the Seraphim, those highest of these angels who, seated before God himself, sing "Holy, Holy, Holy" in praise of the glory of the Creator. This realm, also known as The Kingdom of Devas, includes all of the traditional angels, from archangels such as Michael, Gabriel, and Raphael to the lesser angels usually referred to as fairies, undines, and nature spirits who support our world in their various ways.

Unlike many, my observations of these magnificent beings who radiate great and beautiful light, do not, I'm sorry to say, include the angelic wings of Renaissance art and culture. I have always recognised their presence by their various shimmering colours: metallic yellows, blues, gold, silver, reds, greens and purple violets.

These entities are like engineers of light. They prepare spaces for sacred work, assist in prayer, healing and meditation, and sustain the invisible forces that form into material objects in our world. As I indicated in an earlier book of mine, *Auras and Colours*, I often used to see the fairy-like smaller varieties of elemental or nature spirits, glowing in a whole range of colours around the flowers and plants at the bottom of my childhood garden. It is a powerful memory of a profound awakening for me.

I also remember how I first noticed that upon entering a room in which I was going to give a lecture, usually on a subject of a psycho-spiritual nature such as healing or meditation, several of these great angels were already present in the space, having helped to prepare the best possible environment for what was going to take place that day. I always acknowledge and thank them, and often mention it to those students present at the time. It is indeed a glorious sight to behold.

Other angels

In this vast infinite cosmos there are other types of beings, which we may encounter from time to time. Like us, they are spiritual beings but they do not fit into the categories mentioned in this book. They may originate from other solar and star systems, other universes, having mastered space, time and travel in ways we have yet to understand. Like the traditional angels, they may not be human in our worldly sense, but they are conscious, intelligent and loving creatures who are interested in what we do here. Just as we have become more globally focussed over the last few centuries, able to travel around the planet with increasing ease and speed, some beings I had contact with explained to me that they have developed a greater awareness of the universe and its laws. Their presence, whatever form it may take, and their purpose is to touch us and even communicate with us here when we have evolved sufficiently to understand them. To travel and visit us is no different for them than for you and I to travel by plane to another continent, only the journey they make is even simpler, as it is primarily a mental one.

I am aware of such beings and have always found their contact friendly, wise and caring. To reach the levels of awareness they have attained, they needed to develop a spiritual maturity of an exceptionally sophisticated order. They have learned to value and cherish life in all its forms wherever they may find it, including we seemingly primitive humans on the planet earth. Evolved non-human beings are always angels of love and wisdom, understanding that God or Divinity exists in all of us, in everything, and that all life should be respected and honoured. That is my experience of all such angels.

Contacting your angels

It is natural for us to have contact with our invisible angels, whatever type they may be, so long as it is done in a spirit of love, humility and wonder, and not idle curiosity, sensation seeking, or a means of massaging our egos. This was certainly the practice amongst the early Christians. For example, contemporary writers of the time such as Tertullian and St. Paul list the "discernment of spirits" along with healing as "gifts of the spirit," both as important aspects of early Christian practice.

Research reveals that all ancient cultures believed in contact and respect of our departed ancestors in some form or another. In the rest of this chapter I will outline some simple suggestions as to how you may honour and acknowledge those who love and support you from their lives and existences in higher realms. This in no way can or should replace the important guidance and training necessary for serious work in this field from an experienced individual teacher with well-honed clairvoyant ability and sound knowledge of spiritual and psychic practices, including appropriate forms of prayer, meditation and mental discipline. I do wish to emphasise this point and encourage the earnest seekers who wish to take their knowledge and interest further to find good support and mentoring. It is vital and will prevent unnecessary problems that may occur along the way. Such practice takes discipline and patience, not to mention hard work. Whilst such teachers are not easy to find—and many will claim that they are such teachers—a good reputation travels. I find that the old maxim "When the pupil is ready the teacher will appear" to be a reliable one. My teachers found me.

Loved ones

For those people you have loved and who have passed through, there are some simple things you can do to remember them and acknowledge their presence.

First remember they still exist, and come close to you at times. Thank them for their love and nearness to you, for all they gave to you and still do. Speak to them in your own words, either out loud in a normal way, just as if they are with you, or silently inside your heart. Always communicate from your heart as if your lips are there and your voice rises from it.

Blessing

Blessing is simply a loving acknowledgement of the gift of something or someone for you. Take a quiet moment, sit in stillness, relax and breathe deeply for a while. Then think of those you love in the higher life and give thanks for them. Say, "I bless you, love you, and thank you." It is often said that we don't know what we've got 'til it's gone, so focus on your heart as you tell them how you valued them and still do and wish them well in their new life. Never say goodbye but rather, "See you later," or something similar. When your life tasks are done you will meet them again.

Anniversaries

The birthdays and passing-on anniversaries of our loved ones are special and should be remembered. Not the pain of an unpleasant illness which in some cases took their life, but a celebration that they have gone on, now pain-free and liberated into a happier place than before. On such occasions you can perhaps place a few flowers around a small candle lit in their honour, and have a favourite photograph of them with you to celebrate their life. You may shed a tear or two, but that is a fine and sometimes natural thing to do. Have a glass of their favourite drink or tea, eat some cake they loved, and remember the good things they did and tried to do. They were likely not a saint, but with all their human failings they did the best they could manage in their life. And they loved you and live on still in another world. Take a few moments to celebrate and give thanks for that. Then go on with the rest of your day. It is what we should do, not speak about them in embarrassed, hushed tones.

The not so loved angels!

A friend of mine had a difficult relationship with his mother, and after she died he was rather surprised that she looked through, saying she loved him and added that she wanted to help him. My experience suggests that even our greatest adversaries visit us to say they are sorry and want to help us if they can. After passing, we appear to develop a broader perspective of our earthly lives and see things more clearly than when we were here. Grudges, dislikes, and even hatred evaporate, so we are free from them it seems. Sometimes the most difficult people in our lives are our greatest teachers, taking on a role that we don't understand at the time or perhaps never entirely do. Someone has to play the bad guy. But in such cases again we should take note of that greatest of teachers who said we must love those who seem to hate us by loving our enemies too.

We are all God's children, none of us perfect. When we recall those we found difficult or maybe downright hostile in their attitudes toward us, we should think and speak through our hearts and bless them, wishing them well in their new journey. That is love in action, true forgiveness, the greatest gift we can give to another, whichever world they live in.

A home blessing

In addition to our ancestor angels, we should also honour and acknowledge the great beings of light or "traditional" angels I mentioned earlier. House blessing is one way to do this. You can do this alone, or with family or a few friends.

Arrange a time when you will be undisturbed. Maybe light a candle to symbolize the light of truth, love, and peace. Relax by breathing slowly and deeply for a while, perhaps playing gentle, quiet music for a few moments, focussing upon your hearts as you do. Place a small vase of flowers near to you or in the centre of the room.

Then invoke or call the angels of peace and love to be with you. (No doubt they already are present but a welcoming invitation brings them and their beautiful light closer to you.) Use words such as, "We welcome the Angels of Light, Love, Wisdom, and Peace to be with us and within this house now and always. We thank you for your presence and the joyful peace you bring to us."

This can be spoken slowly, gently, and out loud. Then relax into the moments, reflecting for a while on these most magnificent of God's workers and builders. If you call them in such a way they will be there with you always, whether you see them or not. Invite them often either formally or in odd moments when you think of doing so. You may well feel them as a warm, soft embrace or even in the sweet scent of flowers that they may bring to you. Some people even hear angel-like bell sounds—I often did as a boy. Enjoy this new relationship with the bringers of God's Great Light, and always thank them for coming.

Fairies and nature spirits

Spring and summer are especially good for this type of contact. The energy of the planet rises and nature awakens into a celebration of growth, making our little unseen friends more active: but they are at work all times of the year, in all weather and all seasons. They direct and encourage the forces and energies of nature to work, like mechanics would service your car to help it to continue running smoothly. They understand the magic of God's natural architecture perfectly.

Take a stroll around your garden, a park, or a forest. Or hike a mountain to a lake or river. Observe the beauty of the plant life and trees. Consider the clear sparkle of the water or the rushing movement of a stream. Pause for a while and imagine these silent angel workers, busily pursuing their varied tasks. If you feel a little crazy doing this at first, remember that you were much more open to these things when you were a child and may even have seen or heard them as I did. But you are in good company here, as more people may do this than you realize. I'm one of them.

Sit for a while and soak up the energy of the moment. Breathe it in slowly and reflect on these wonderful nature and water spirits. Thank them and bless them in your own words and share your heart with them. It is a joy many of us have lost, and that some have yet to know, but one we should all seek and savour in this busy world. It is healing if you can sit or lie next to a great tree or flowers, inhale slowly for a while and allow the energy given you to nourish you and bring you peace, love and a deepening sense of connection to life.

Just watch how well your garden flowers thrive when you do this from time to time.

Your guides

For the development of contact with your personal guides, or, if you prefer, guardian angels, a simple ritual is useful. For many years I took a regular time each week, plus other odd moments I could manage, to open a very deep and trusting contact, which has been pivotal in my life. It is based on love and trust and a sincere desire for the relationship to be for the highest good for me and everyone I am associated with. As I mentioned earlier, for in-depth work with guides a mentor or knowledgeable teacher is important to avoid delusional and bad practices. But you can commence the process simply by yourself.

Regularly find a quiet place that is peaceful and still, away from mobile phones and other distractions. If indoors, light a candle and dedicate your connection with a simple opening prayer. Keep a notepad and pen near to you. Use words such as, "I dedicate this time to acknowledging my highest guidance and to those of God's workers who seek to guide and help me to serve and follow my true path of unfoldment in light, love and understanding. Thank you for being with me." As you look at the candlelight, imagine the spiritual light that shines in you and from you like a beacon.

Breathe slowly, and again maybe have a small vase of flowers nearby whilst playing some gentle music. After a while relax further, quiet or turn off the music completely, and reflect on the Higher Guides or High Angels as they are usually termed, who are with you from birth until death.

Stay for a period in calm meditation, continuing to breathe quietly and peacefully. After a few sessions of this you may feel the atmosphere around you soften and warm. Simply relax into it for a while.

Return slowly to normal consciousness, awakening gently and enjoying another moment or two of stillness before thanking your invisible angelic visitors for being with you, even if at first you are not especially aware of them. At this point you can again imagine that you are full of beautiful radiant light, then fully ground yourself by feeling your feet firmly in contact with the floor and opening closed eyes. Be patient and trusting, and always dedicate what you do to "The Highest Good."

If you feel inspired afterwards, write a few words down, read a poem or page from a book. Unfolding guidance of any spiritual type will often inspire you creatively. It may well be a first sign that you are actually receiving guidance and it will be surprisingly appropriate for that moment whatever words you read or write. If you are an artist or musician you will eventually be inspired to explore those gifts more and more.

Remember, patience, sincerity, love, and humility are the keys to these connections.

And always ask for help and guidance, whatever the situation. If not immediately, it will surely always come.

Such practices can change your life in the most wonderful ways. I assure you they will.

For he shall give his angels charge over thee, to keep thee in all thy ways. Psalm 91:11 King James Bible.

CHAPTER 12

The Aura Angel and My Eureka Moment

～≋～

So far I have largely described what has happened for others in some of the many sessions I've conducted and what I've observed and learned from them. The following pages, however, tell a different story concerning a series of my own experiences—vital ones, important in my unfoldment and understanding that enhanced my ability to help others.

I met an important angel

The young woman entered my practice room, wearing a broad rather self-satisfied smile. Waving a couple of pages she had taken from a Sunday newspaper colour supplement magazine a day or so before, she sat on the chair in front of me as she usually did, legs crossed, staring at me intently.

"Guess what I've found?" she asked.

"Come on. Put me out of my misery, Claire," I replied.

"Look, Paul." She paused, just as a parent would when gently teasing a child before it is finally given the present they are holding in front of them. "It's an article about an artist." She then thrust the pages into my hands grinning as she did so.

Claire was a young woman in her early thirties. I taught her meditation and other mental strategies so she could gain confidence and a sense of purpose. I saw her regularly to help with her anxiety issues and to offer guidance and direction by observing her aura. As I previously mentioned, an aura is a field of light and energy that radiates around all living and inanimate objects, which can reveal much about us. I have seen the phenomenon of the aura since childhood, studied it, and learned how to interpret the information it reveals. This ability had enabled me to help Claire and support many others, becoming a main aspect of my work over the past few decades.

There were several illustrations on the second page of the magazine article, two of them providing a "eureka!" moment for me. One photograph was of a painting by Kandinsky, an artist with whom I have a particular connection and in whom I have a special interest. But it was the illustration next to it that really caught my eye. It was taken from a book written by the late Theosophist teacher and clairvoyant C. W. Leadbeater, depicting a human aura. I felt the energy rise in me as I examined it more closely.

"It is similar to the drawings you do, isn't it?" she said observing my smiling face.

"At last, someone who sees auras very much as I do. That's brilliant. Well spotted!"

I was absolutely delighted. I had checked with many books and writers on the subject of the aura over many years but I had not seen an illustration that resembled my own perception of this vibrant field until this moment.

C. W. Leadbeater had been only vaguely familiar to me. Some time ago I'd been given one of his books, but had only glanced through it. I have always worked deductively, learning to trust what I saw clairvoyantly even though initially I often didn't understand exactly what it was. Then I do what research I can, absorbing ideas and theories to see what it may be that my clairvoyant vision was revealing to me. Here, at last, was a picture of the human aura that closely resembled my own view—not exactly, but very similar.

I had long been aware that my aura work was guided as I sought to unravel the mystery of these layers of beautifully coloured light emanating not only from all living things, but also from the inanimate objects of the material world. Until this point, the identity of that angel guide had been unknown to me. This article revealed that there existed someone who, in his astounding life on this earth, shared closely my current perception of subtle auric light and forces. I had no idea of his significance to me at that point, but it set me on a path that led to many fascinating discoveries. The artist Kandinsky added yet another significant link.

My drawings and paintings were not only aids to help me understand what I saw; they were also an important prelude to my meeting a most important angel who guided my work. Many years ago, when training as a painter, I had an exhibition of my work hung for final assessment. The assessor walked among the pictures of all the final year students, including a selection of my own work that my tutor and I had chosen. I waited anxiously for her to interview me. I remember how nervous I felt; the other students seemed to me much more talented than I was, exhibiting, in my opinion, some wonderful work. When she came over to me to examine more closely my paintings, my sketches and working drawings, she first paused at some watercolours. Her glance then fixed firmly on my larger oil and acrylic works.

"Do you know the work of the artist Kandinsky?" she asked.

I can't recall exactly what I muttered, but it was along the lines of, "I've heard of him." I had indeed heard of him but knew little else at that time.

"You're work is very much like his," she replied, politely ignoring my ignorance.

Much later, I was to discover that Kandinsky was involved with the Theosophical movement, in which C. W. Leadbeater was a leading figure, hence the link in the article between the two men. Kandinsky could also see auras, as is suggested in some of his paintings such as *Woman in Moscow, Lady in Moscow* and many of his more abstract works. Kandinsky also wrote on the relationship between art and spirituality, as he saw thought forms and light fields, the stunning lights observed by clairvoyant vision. Some of my paintings revealed my own similar perception of these phenomena. I didn't know at that time what it was I saw, and that they were auras. I simply realised I perceived these things and wanted to paint them, as they seemed a more interesting subject matter than a still life of apples, chianti bottles, or the nude models I had endeavoured to paint, often badly. This special angel relationship and its significance, just beginning to unfold at that time, were to prove exciting for me.

Not long after Claire had enlightened me with the Kandinsky article, I had an important angel visitor. I was at home one evening. After a long telephone chat with a relative I felt a little tired, so I relaxed in the armchair. The rest of the family had gone up to bed and I welcomed the opportunity of some time alone to reflect on the events of what had been a busy day.

As I settled, a voice called, "Paul, Paul, I am here. Recognise me?" In front of me I could see a distinguished looking man in white clothing, grey/white hair and a beard, radiating a soft warm smile.

It was one of those strange moments when you recognise someone, but don't know why you do, nor can you identify him or her. Yet I somehow knew this angel. His appearance was familiar, very familiar, but I couldn't place this figure. "Think back. I will help you if you wish."

I did try to "think back" but, with no immediate success. I couldn't place the face of this angel or put a name to it, no matter how much I tried to do so. He then disappeared and it was some time before I was to discover his identity.

Then one weekend I was lecturing on a healing course at the Theosophical Society venue Tekels Park in Surrey. In the main building was a room of occult books. In a free moment I was able to speak to the woman in charge, and she invited me into that room, which proved to be a treasure house. Examining a few editions and turning over a few covers, I saw a photograph, which made me gasp. Gazing back up at me was my angel visitor. It was C. W. Leadbeater.

Over the coming months, from what appeared to be various unconnected sources who knew nothing of my newly aroused interest in this figure, books from his authorship were given or sent to me, completely unsolicited. One man who was a student of mine at the time, commented, "I don't know why, I thought you might be interested in this."

There were many visits from this angel in the following years, and I became accustomed to his wise counsel and gentle advice, particularly when looking at individual auras and subtle energy fields, seeking to interpret them efficiently. A deeply significant relationship with this invisible angel was developing.

A corporate psychic

Viewing the aura became an increasing fascination, which gradually evolved into the central element of my work. I still taught meditation, practised as a healer, wrote, and lectured on various psycho-spiritual matters. However, the fields of light dominated much of my research and reflections. And the angel C. W., as I began to refer to him, was a great blessing and an increasing influence. This became especially apparent when a businessman I knew slightly, approached me and asked if I would work for him on a regular basis in return for a paid monthly retainer fee.

He had originally consulted me on his wife's suggestion, wanting advice on a key appointment he sought to make in his company, a manufacturing business with a presence in several countries. He told me he was aware that I was frequently asked to look at candidates for all manner of management roles. What had impressed him most was my ability to perceive the colours and frequencies of an individual's aura clearly, whether the individual was physically with me or not, and to give a detailed assessment of their abilities and suitability for a senior position. Clearly, this was a useful talent for his needs.

I never meet the individual candidates, and rarely see their CV or resume. I simply have their name and the particular roles for which they are being considered. It may be finance director, head of research and development, marketing manager, or general manager of a subsidiary branch of the business.

Like anyone with well-developed psychic abilities, I study the aura of each candidate, making notes, attempting to provide a written evaluation of the candidates' strengths, including if they are ready for a new challenge and fresh opportunity that the job offers, and whether they would fit into the company culture effectively.

Needless to say, it is vital and in the best interests of all concerned, that my assessments are accurate. I have learned there is always, ultimately, a "right man/woman" for the role. With a company's future success at stake, along with someone's career and possibly the jobs of many others, I strive to be thorough, checking and re-checking the information I have gleaned from a candidate's aura.

C. W. proved to be an enormous help, particularly when I encountered a situation when it was not clear to me, which was the most suitable candidate. In those moments, C. W. helped me by drawing my attention again to a particular element or quality I needed to emphasize, or reassuring me that I made the right choice. This was especially useful when other consultative advice the company received on the matter differed from my own view.

On one occasion, we were looking for a general manager for a new manufacturing plant in Eastern Europe. There were several male candidates and one woman. The conventional view would have been with an almost completely male workforce, a male appointment would be obvious. There were several strong male applicants, and other consulting agencies also advising the company, supported one of them for the position.

However, my own assessment put the woman candidate at the top of the list by quite some margin. Whilst I was secure in my opinion, it would not have surprised me if she was overlooked, despite my advice. In a moment of reflection on the matter, I felt C. W.'s presence. He advised me that it was the best solution. He helped me to look at the character of the woman again, to review her aura, further strengthening in my mind what I had already concluded. I could see she was resolute and determined, loyal, detail oriented, and possessed the necessary interpersonal skills to manage a team in a large factory—whatever their gender.

The woman was appointed and has proved effective and successful in managing the factory with its male workforce in a sophisticated manufacturing environment. (This story was referred to in an article in the business section of the London based *Sunday Times* in May 2012).

Finer details

Understandably some may ask, why would such an elevated being as C. W. Leadbeater be at all interested in something as mundane as advising me on filling jobs in a business? It is not an easy question to answer without putting this angel's help and guidance to me into the broader context of how our relationship has grown. In rare situations the shared and persistent interest in a subject will naturally lead to a deep collaboration between the angel and the one being mentored. As in any relationship, trust, respect and profound understanding between the two develop over time as it has with us, covering a wide range of connected themes and ideas. In such situations there are moments of profound symbiosis.

First and most obvious is C. W.'s helping me to teach, write, and help thousands of people through my developing knowledge of the aura and subtle, invisible forces. "We" have readers and clients and students all over the world who benefit from our collaboration.

Secondly, I was brought up Roman Catholic as a child, and C. W.'s guidance has helped me to make sense of some of the forces and streams of light my psychic abilities allowed me to see at the Mass or Eucharist in church on Sundays. I saw what appeared to be non-human beings, radiating the most beautiful colours, especially in the sanctuary around the altar at the consecration of the bread and wine. C. W. has helped me to understand these are the conventional angels, wingless in my view, but magnificent and powerful architects of light and beautiful forces. His book, *Science of the Sacraments*, which was also sent to me out of the blue by a student, was a critical help in my growing understanding.

Thirdly, he helps me observe the subtle processes underway in my students, clients and patients who come to me for healing. This is vital in my adapting more effectively to the needs of the moment.

Fourthly, and perhaps the most vital to my work overall, is the manner in which C. W. often appears when I am considering other spiritual matters. This is particularly useful when I look (and am shown) clairvoyantly how energy and particles, atoms and other invisible substances around us (the "chitta" or "mind stuff" of the Hindus) behave, interact and form clusters or groups which in turn build what we perceive as the physical objects of our three dimensional world. It also shows me how our thoughts and feelings ultimately shape our reality. His advice is a major blessing as I unravel the meanings of what I observe.

The fact that C. W. was well known in his field is of little consequence to me or for me. He still has a mission to help and inspire humanity, and his wise support of me is a part of that task.

Like all high angel visitors, he guides and helps, *but he does not dictate to me.* He encourages me to see in my own way and work things out for myself. I have my own opinions and whilst in some respects our clairvoyance is similar, there are many differences. He admits to me that he was not always completely right; and like all clairvoyants, we don't see everything. Equally, there is no such thing, from a human perspective, as absolute objectivity. We all see things differently, whether with our physical vision or our inner, clairvoyant eye. But this angel's support is an invaluable gift to me in my own deliberations and much of the work I still do.

Why so familiar?

As related earlier, when I first saw C. W., he seemed familiar. Subsequent viewings of pictures and photographs of him simply reinforced and confirmed this strong impression. But how he was so known to me remained a puzzle. Then, as we say, the penny dropped.

I recount in an earlier book of mine, *Auras and Colours*, what I believe to be a pre-birth memory. It is a clear vision of a time just before I was born into this physical life. The memory included being with several figures whom, again, I did not know but who were strangely familiar to me—just like when we meet people for the first time, yet we feel we already know them. That is how I felt about these figures as I waited to emerge into this world.

Suddenly, in a moment of powerful insight, all the threads of connection came together. As I prepared for birth, the identity of one of the figures became clear to me. It was C. W. Leadbeater, a true Angel of spiritual science and a great blessing to me.

I'm sure I felt him smile.

CHAPTER 13

Angels in Times of Great Crisis

*In a moment of crisis we can feel quite alone. Even if others are around us physically, we may still experience a peculiar isolation when something in our lives goes badly wrong, either for us personally or for someone close to us. This can be particularly true of bereavement.

I remember a man speaking to me of the time his mother died when he was a teenager. He had no belief in an afterlife of any kind and his relationship with his businessman father was not an especially close one. He felt completely alone and upon going out into the street shortly after her death, he couldn't understand why everyone else was behaving normally, continuing to go about their daily lives while he was experiencing a great personal tragedy. He wanted to scream out to those passing by, "Don't you know my mum has just died?"

These feelings are not unusual in the moments of shock that accompany painful episodes. Anyone who has had an accident will comprehend this sense of being cut off from life. However brief it may be, for a while it seems nobody cares or appreciates our predicament. We are alone in a strange world trying to cope with our feelings, wanting our distress to be understood by those around us, but that rarely seems to happen.

The same can be said when someone miles from home is seriously or even fatally injured and their loved ones are not yet aware or able to be there to comfort them. They are alone.

But what about our invisible friends? Are they there?

It is clear to me that they are: relatives and loved ones from the next worlds often surround the bed of a dying man, ready to assist him adjust once he has left his physical body. I have seen this many times. Several years ago I was waiting at the counter in a pub, ordering some drinks for my friends when the man next to me suddenly collapsed onto the floor. He was still alive but unconscious, taking short, snatched breaths, as he lay there almost motionless. Fortunately, there was a doctor nearby who quickly diagnosed that he had suffered a stroke.

What struck me at the time was how aware I became of other invisible beings around him. Several of them were in attendance, though I had no idea who they were—angels of some kind, perhaps deceased loved ones, coming to him in his time of acute need. I also recall the beautiful, shimmering light that appeared, wrapping the man in a cloak of rose peach splendour accompanied by an unusual calm, despite the concern and activity around him as an ambulance was summoned and the doctor knelt by his side, holding his hand. This radiance was the kind of metallic glow I witnessed as a child, when I could see the traditional angels around the altar in the church, managing and preparing the appropriate invisible forces according to the needs of the moment—the engineers of light as they seem to be. In this man's crisis he was being helped, of that I have no doubt.

This is just one of many stories of this kind. But what of massive events involving many people, catastrophes with global impacts? Are our angels able to cope then? Why should we doubt that?

9/11

This horrific event is etched in the minds of most of us, whether or not we were directly involved. One interesting aspect of the events surrounding 9/11 is the large number of people who subsequently reported having a precognitive vision of or dream of such a tragedy in the preceding days. Although I was not one who received such visions, my daughter was. However, as with everyone else I have researched on this matter, there were no specific details in her premonition as to exactly where or when it would take place, or whom it might involve.

I recall the day clearly. The television was switched on in our lounge at home and immediately scenes of the unfolding carnage were shown in what became continuous emergency news coverage. A client who was intending to fly from Dublin to see me that day called saying that all flights were grounded, so she wouldn't be coming.

What I became aware of clairvoyantly was both remarkable and stunning, even to a believer and worker in the higher realms as I was. Equally, as a human being I was not immune to feeling shocked and completely helpless in those moments.

As the first plane struck, the whole area around the cluster of towered buildings was bathed in a vibrant yellow gold light, stunning and radiant. In this coloured field were hundreds of smaller sparkling lights. These are the spheres many psychics see when angel visitors of various kinds first appear to them, often referred to as "spirit lights." I have no doubt that among these angels were the relatives of those who were killed immediately, helping them cope with their sudden and traumatic arrival into a new dimension. Other angels did what they could to help the injured and the terrified, even though they were probably unaware of that help. It is always given, whether we know it or not.

By the time of the second strike the light around the area had expanded, now including the rose colour of love and affection, along with the gold of wisdom and understanding. The number of angel visitors must have grown to thousands. There was enormous spiritual activity underway.

Then I saw the souls, or spirits, of those who died being accompanied by angel lights, taken away from the environment of the towers, lifted clear of the mayhem to the calm of another place. They were in groups, appearing to fly through the air. This really was a case of choirs of angels in action. Perhaps even more surprising was the sight of those who decided to jump to their deaths. I saw them being lifted from their physical bodies by angel lights before they crashed to the ground below.

This rather confirms my personal experience of near death, and the fact that we, our spiritual selves, depart from our physical bodies very quickly at the point of death, often before we have clinically died. In such moments our attachment to our physical self is just enough to sustain a robotic or so-called "vegetative" state but no more. We no longer feel anything through our nervous system, and we can, if we choose, let go of our body and let it cease to function in an instant as these souls were doing. As a shocked observer, I found this sight reassuring and affirming: that even in the most awful crises, we are never alone and receive unfailing angel support.

It is worth reminding the reader that clairvoyants can not only look forward to the future, but also backward in time, which is why I can give such a detailed account. It is a fourth dimensional faculty so it is possible for a psychic to tune in to observe what happened in the past at a higher dimensional level just as we can watch a film of past physical events. I can look at an old photo of an individual and see their coloured aura as it was at the time the photograph was taken and also how it looks now. All good psychics can do this. Equally I can watch a film report and do the same, so I was able to review the events of 9/11 several times to witness what was happening at the higher as well as the physical levels.

We tend to learn from our mistakes

Some will of course ask why did our angels not prevent those who died from being there in the first place or even stop the whole attack from happening?

There is the matter of free will. We have choices and the angels are not able to interfere with that principle. Of course, if we are able and willing to listen they will advise us, perhaps warning us of an impending tragedy or unnecessary accident. But ultimately, we on the earth still tend to learn by our mistakes, shaping our own destinies, individually and collectively. In such times they will help us cope with the consequences of our actions, so we may learn whatever we may need to learn, not making the same mistakes again.

In any crisis, even something as shocking as the attack on the twin towers, at a higher level something wonderful is happening. And whether individually or collectively, whether on the battle field or in a car crash, the angels of all kinds are there for us, helping when we are ready to be helped; assuaging our pain and guiding us perfectly as only God's messengers can do.

CHAPTER 14

What Angels Really
Tell Us

*In this book I have recounted stories selected from thousands like them—stories that I have been fortunate enough to participate in over a lifetime. These stories underscore that such communications from angel messengers are a common phenomenon. There are thousands of us psychics and mediumistic individuals of excellent caliber all over the world acting as intermediaries between those who have "died" and those still here, for whom we bring healing, comfort, hope and understanding. I think such contact with higher worlds is a wonderfully natural process, which, as I have said, many either never knew or have forgotten was possible. Or perhaps they have shunned it, neglected it through prejudice and fear, or sought to ignore or even condemn it.

So, what is the point? Many of the messages are simple, ordinary in content, bringing back everyday memories of times once shared—birthdays, anniversaries, favourite cakes granny or mother used to make, thanks for the loving care and support given during a final illness—moving and full of meaning for the recipient, but perhaps considered banal and not especially interesting to the casual observer. What are these messengers and their messages really telling us? Following are some conclusions I have arrived at based upon my years of experience.

A life beyond here

Perhaps the most obvious point is that there is more than we realise to life and what we call death. Somehow the personality continues after dying and some souls, in the appropriate circumstances, are able to communicate that to us here on earth. While there is no such thing as absolute proof of anything, since methods of proof are a construct of the intellect in its reductionist frenzy, the evidence that I and other mediums can attest to, drawn from our work with many individuals suggests something significant about the continuity of life, in whatever form, beyond this material world.

Others have argued that such contacts are illusions created for the gullible and needy, or an act of superb mind reading. But repeatedly angel messengers provide information that neither the psychic nor the recipient knows at the time, or could possibly know, only discovering it to be true later. "Your father's had a fall. He's okay, but call home when you can," came one message to a client from her departed mum. Thirty minutes later she called home to find that the fall in the garden her father had taken was fortunately not too serious. It had occurred whilst she was speaking with me and received the angel's message. By any standards, that is some impossible feat of human mind reading and quite an illusion! And a lucky guess? Such things happen far too often for that to be true. The degree of collusion necessary, implicit in such criticisms, would be of such magnitude, sometimes involving people who don't even know each other at the time of the event, that it would be impossible to orchestrate, let alone carry off effectively.

Somehow, we continue after death. What a message that is for us all.

Purpose in the afterlife

Whilst our angels find it difficult to explain exactly what they are up to in the next world, they seem no longer to be preoccupied with coping with physical disease, economic survival, and all the many material concerns we have here. To us, it would seem like paradise. A perpetual holiday!

In the communications I have been a witness to, one message comes through: A purposeful existence continues after physical death even though the details reported on the exact nature of that new life are filled with activities we may find very difficult if not impossible to comprehend.

Again I can state that I have yet to hear of harp playing or floating on clouds, though I suspect if we really wanted to, we could give it a try. What is presented instead is a dynamic state of being in which our minds are employed purposefully and creatively in meaningful tasks. Life appears to be a continuum of some kind, a never ending story, and this existence is merely one episode in its telling. It would also appear that we experience many lifetimes, throughout the planet's history, as a part of our journey. This in itself poses some further interesting questions such as, do we always incarnate in the same gender? The readings I have given over the years suggest (as referenced in Chapter 4) we can be of either sex. Do we have lives in different countries and continents in different periods of history? Again, the messages I have witnessed on this matter imply that we do. Life appears to be a remarkable adventure through space and time for us all.

Do we hold them back?

A common criticism of those of us seeking angel communication is that in so doing we hold their spirits back, inhibiting their progress and binding them to the earth they have left behind; that our need to talk to them, and know that they are okay is somehow selfish and limiting for them. These contacts reveal that is simply not true. No one can "summon up the dead" as it was once put to me. It seems that in the next life they are able to be the ultimate multi-tasker, capable of doing something inconceivable to those of us still firmly anchored in this physically dense world. Time and space as we know them no longer restrict them as they do us—they can be in more than one place at what appears to be the same time.

The consistency and frequency of this message is borne out by the research of Dr. Gary Schwartz in his Veritas project at the University of Arizona mentioned earlier, where he and his staff methodically examined the work of many experienced psychics and mediums. We cannot hold angels back. They communicate because they choose to do so and repeatedly demonstrate their abilities to be engaged in more than one activity at a time— what a useful skill that would be here on earth.

In fact, our angel friends often show great determination to alert someone with an active psychic nature such as a medium, of their presence and their desire to make contact. The appearance of the monks in Chapter 10 whilst I was dining in a restaurant is a good example. Equally, if someone in the next world does not want contact with us, they won't do it. I have occasionally had a client with me who wished to communicate with a particular angel. So often in these cases, many family and friend angels visit us, but not the one they had desperately wanted to hear from. There can be many reasons why this happens, not the least being the intense emotional desire of the client acting as a psychic barrier to the contact, like static electricity affecting a phone line, or it may simply not be the right time. Yet on a later occasion they meet with success and the loved one appears.

A friend of mine died and promised to contact his wife after death, she herself being a medium. Despite visiting several other mediums and psychics she heard no evidence of his presence and was consequently very saddened. She gave up trying, then one afternoon some years later I was having tea with her, when quite suddenly, I was aware of her late husband. She had never asked me for help in the matter, as she preferred to seek contact through someone who had never known her husband and could be as objective as possible. He showed me the number 21. Then he held up a ballerina figurine seeking to give it to his wife, saying there was something unusual about her skirt. I was puzzled and had no idea what he meant, but as I told this to his widow she cried, abruptly leaving the room only to return minutes later holding a porcelain figure. It was a ballerina wearing a cotton and lace ballet dress. It had been a present to her from her husband Charles on her twenty-first birthday. He took his time to come through but did eventually, when it was right for him to do so.

Humour

Spiritual matters are so often treated as solemn, requiring excessive gravitas. A visit to some churches may confirm this where there is much fear or solemnity evident but not always much joy. Of course there is a time and place for everything, and that includes tranquil reflection and deep, thoughtful moments. But, much to my relief, it would appear from my contact with our angels, they don't lose their sense of humour and perhaps, by inference, neither should we. I often tell clients not to forget the moments of laughter they enjoyed with their departed loved ones, and not to dwell too much on the difficulties. These visitors all tell us that they are pain-free, clear of the disease that caused their death and are not slow to remind us of the humour and even sauciness they once shared with us, as the conversations in Chapter 8 reveal.

They can help us to help ourselves

The angels can help us, encourage us, guide us a little, a bit like giving clues in a quiz, and even warn us of extreme dangers we might avoid. But they have to allow us our own freedom to discover, learn, and grow for ourselves. They cannot and will not take over our lives for us and neither should they. This is sometimes referred to as the Law or Principle of Non-Interference; if we ask for help it will be given to us, but then only as support and guidance or we would be nothing more than slaves, seriously compromising our free will. I remember one lady becoming angry with the angels and me when they declined her request to select a lawyer to manage her impending divorce.

We are ultimately responsible for our time here, our thoughts, words and deeds. They cannot take that away from us and neither will true angels seek to do that.

We are not alone

This planet can be a very lonely place at times. Even when we are surrounded by people, we can still feel an inner loneliness. There are reasons for that which are not within the scope of this book. What we should remember is that the presence of these angels serves as a constant reminder that we are never alone, if we don't wish to be. They are not spying on us like some invisible spiritual voyeur. I recall my youngest son, once asking how it was they seemed able to see us wherever we are. I told him about my near death experience when I was struck by lightning as a teenager, and how I could see through what were to us on earth, solid forms. He paused and thought for a while before asking, "Can they even see us in the toilet?"

I assured him that in the higher life they have better things to do than worry about that. However, we should always remember we have invisible help and comfort should we wish it. I recall how the former British hostage, John McCarthy, described in the book, *Some Other Rainbow*, which he co-authored with his then girlfriend, Jill Morrell, how desperately lonely he became during his long captivity in Beirut. He was kept in darkened isolation and felt his position was futile. Suddenly, in his darkest moment, although he was not especially a spiritual man, he called out to God. Then, he felt and saw a presence in the form of a bright light which calmed him, gave him renewed optimism and he was able to endure his remaining days in captivity with more fortitude and hope. John said he did not know who or what it was. He called it the Good Spirit. I suggest it was a visiting angel, helping him to feel that he was not alone.

Always remember that you need never be alone if you do not wish to be.

Our loved ones are still interested in us

It is clear that when they have gone into the higher life, our angels, former friends and loved ones, do not lose interest in us. They watch over us in a kind benevolent way, keeping in touch with us if they can, if or when we give them the opportunity to do so. My pal Rob's mum communicated to me that she cared about him, long after her death, even though their relationship had not been an easy one when she was here. He was pleasantly surprised that it was so. It seems when we are no longer here we develop a broader, more tolerant perspective so that the prejudices and pettiness that govern so much of our relationships dissolve away.

A father, who had passed over while his son was still at school, gave him the message, "I am so happy for you that you got your degree. Well done. Am so proud." The young man's eyes filled with tears when I told him this and he realised his beloved Pop was still interested in his life and achievements.

There is no "out of sight, out of mind" as far as angels are concerned.

We are met when we pass through

Most of us fear death. We will all experience death at some point, but in Western society at least, we don't like to talk about it. If we are inclined to do so, we often speak in hushed tones as we mention the unmentionable. It is the process itself we usually fear, that final illness many of us endure before leaving this temporary body, unless we are lucky enough to die peacefully and quickly in our sleep.

Angel communications continually tell us that we are accompanied as we pass through. I have experienced this first hand when my great-grandmother met me in my near death experience, telling me to return to my earthly life.

Often those about to pass through will tell those at their bedside they can see this one or that one, usually family members long since passed on before them. Dismissed as hallucination by many, it is more likely that as they prepare to leave their body, they become more aware of where they are going, with a foot in both worlds for a time. As alluded to in an earlier chapter, when my mother was only hours from death, she mentioned many of her former relatives, her brother and sister especially, and her mother, being there with her; Mum slowly pointing towards them at the foot of her bed where I could see them too, waiting for her.

When we pass through, we are met by those angels who knew us here and continue to care for us. We are not left on our own for such an important journey.

Judgement

Some religions promote the idea of a judgement after death, that we are somehow given a scorecard and assessed to how we did in our time here. It is rarely portrayed as a pleasant or healing process. However, angel communications suggest something different, something more in keeping with ancient concepts, as in the various Books of The Dead. It appears that there is indeed some kind of review to help us understand and learn from our earth experience but we are our own judges. For example, in my conversations with angels who committed suicide, they are certainly not punished as some may think (Chapter 6: Suicides and Murders). As one angel commented, many of us on earth are unconsciously committing a kind of suicide much of the time by the manner in which we live our lives, organise our societies, treat our environments and so on. I am inclined to agree. We have a self-destruct default setting.

No one judges us. We are helped to see clearly in order to review and evaluate how we shaped up to our challenges, our trials and tribulations and to learn from how we conducted ourselves in those moments.

Animals survive, too

When my dear old dog, Megan, died a few years ago I was heartbroken. She was my best friend in so many ways—affectionate, loyal and loving, as pets often are. Many of my clients are animal lovers and are also very sad when their pets leave them. "How can those eyes that shone so brightly suddenly grow dim?" as Art Garfunkel's song *Bright Eyes* mournfully echoes.

Well, they live on too, however much that idea may conflict with some religious teachings. I have seen everything from a doted-upon goldfish to a much-loved horse, still existing in the higher life, paying us a visit. My dear dad often appears to me with my beloved Megan at his side. You can be sure that if you had a much loved pet that has died, when you think of them, they are with you and will greet you again one day when you, too, walk through into a new life in another world.

Times are changing, rapidly

This may be obvious to anyone who is abreast of the times. Climate change, social upheaval, financial crises bring us messages of enormous change to our planet, the likes of which we in this world have never witnessed before. What we consider to be reality here is not this solid, immovable, unchangeable box. It is a fluid mass of light and energy, existing within the "many mansions," or possibilities referred to by Jesus in the gospels. Our science now recognises and confirms what metaphysics has long suggested: that we exist in vast fields of subtle matter, particles and light. Our home is a cosmos of infinite possibilities with no limits, no immutable forms. When we are in the higher life, and not loaded down and limited by physical appearances, it seems we are more aware of that truth. Quantum physics affords us a view of that, as the angels that have communicated with me have shown. What we have here on earth will be gone one day like a puff of smoke. The material world continually evolves, but now is moving rapidly. We have to let go and move on, just as those who went before us did when they moved from this world to another, embracing the changes that come.

A sprat to catch a mackerel

A famous healer once said to me that when we have had a few contacts and messages from our departed loved ones through a medium, instead of going back for more, we should ask ourselves some bigger questions. Not those concerning what the content of the messages may have been or even who they were from. Rather we should ask ourselves, "Why did I have this type of contact at all? Why did this happen to me? What does all this mean?"

These experiences are the sprat or small fish used to catch a bigger one. The big one in this case is the drawing of our attention away from the material world to, initially at least, become aware of other invisible realms. In such moments, as we sit with an experienced medium, the subtle energies generated by both them and our angel visitors wash through us, touching us deeply. We may or may not be aware of this happening to us at the time but it surely does, stirring long concealed memories that sleep deep in our subconscious, waiting to be awoken.

To use a metaphor, it is the kiss of the prince awakening the slumbering princess, the princess being our spirit, our essence. It is an opportunity for us to change, to grow and gain fresh perspectives. For many it is the beginning of a search to unfold a greater vision of life and its meaning. For some a completely new life develops and a loved one's death is transmuted into something beautiful, filling them with hope and a stimulating quest for new possibilities. Nearly always the desire to do something wonderful for life emerges.

Clients have often said to me, "You have changed my life!" Flattering though these words may be, I am sufficiently humble to know it is not so. If anything has stimulated positive, creative change in them it is the experience itself.

Our angels teach us that there is so much in the universe that is hidden, the true meaning of the word occult being "not seen." They seek to show us that even if we don't comprehend these invisible worlds and dimensions with the 15% of our brains that we currently utilise, we should open our hearts and minds and let the wonderful child in us explore the reality beyond the limits of mortal senses. There is much to be discovered, especially concerning ourselves. The messages are just a beginning of an adventure. I have witnessed this often, and it is wonderful to see.

Love

Perhaps most of all, our angels tell us about love; a love that gives of itself selflessly; a love that never dies and becomes clearer, more real when we are not boxed in by the limits and petty fears of this earthly life. Time after time, the messages from our angels say, "I love you." They have nothing to gain from those words and the sweet, warm energy in which they are wrapped, except to help us feel that we belong; we belong in this universe; that we matter and always will; that in us they see something special. It is a message that real love never fades. When they are gone from our physical world, we realise, sometimes a bit late that the love of our families, friends, our fellow human beings, and our animals is the most wonderful thing they ever tried to show us. When they visit us as angels, it is their love compelling them to come to us. And that is the most important angel message of all.

"When love beckons to you, follow him, ... and when he speaks to you, believe in him."

The Prophet, by Kahlil Gibran

A Glossary of Useful Terms

angel. A being who has no physical form or body, and in some cases never has, but exists in the higher worlds and is essentially a messenger, or as with traditional angels, exists as a "worker" or "engineer of light" solely dedicated to helping God's mysterious plan on earth.

archangel. Higher level angels, including Michael, Uriel, Metatron, Raphael, who oversee particular purposes or parts of the Divine plan.

aura. The electro-magnetic energy and coloured light fields that radiate around the physical body or three-dimensional form of a human being, animal, plant and all physical objects.

astral body. The esoteric term used to denote the brightly coloured emotional field in the aura. It is also known as the psychic body. It is derived from the Latin word "astra" meaning "stars" and alludes to its bright starry light.

astral plane. The level or plane of being, in which the astral body exists and to where our main mental focus moves after physical death.

clairvoyance. "Clear seeing," or the ability which psychics and mediums possess enabling them to see the subtle or higher worlds, auras and those who have passed into the higher life.

clairaudience. "Clear hearing" that enables the psychic or medium to hear information and voices from higher planes or worlds.

clairsentience. "Clear feeling" where psychic impressions are felt or sensed. Most mediums and psychics use a combination of all three psychic functions.

energy. The invisible substance in which electrical particles vibrate at a rate not visible to all but the edge of the retina in the human eye, and from which all physical matter is formed.

guide. A non-physical being who has usually lived on earth in a physical body and who has the responsibility to support and guide an individual or group as they live out their earthly life. Everyone has a guide or guides, and they are considered by some to be guardian angels. Their role is to help, not control or interfere.

ghost. A residual memory, often an image but sometimes a sound and even a perfume, imprinted into the invisible energy field of a location. It is usually triggered into manifestation by an observer. Its behaviour is always repetitive and similar to all who witness it. Unlike other communicators it is no longer governed in its behaviour by its soul or spiritual essence from which it has become detached like an old garment. Sometimes referred to as an "astral shell."

incarnation. A time or period where the soul or spiritual essence of an individual is present on earth in a physical, carnal or fleshy body.

ley lines. An invisible network of lines of force and energy, which exist in the subtle energy field of the planet, and are sometimes referred to as the planet's nervous system.

lower angels. Nature spirits, fairies, sprites, and elementals.

medium. An individual who has the ability to be the link or "medium" through which beings existing in worlds beyond the physical life can communicate with us.

out of the body experience. The process of consciously leaving the physical body and becoming aware of higher, non-physical levels of experience; sometimes referred to as astral travel.

psychic. Generally means an individual who has a very sensitive and active astral or psychic/emotional body and who is aware of the astral world and its phenomena. Dreams are psychic phenomena and everyone is potentially psychic. Discarnate beings and our departed loved ones often try to communicate with us through our dream state.

rescue medium. A medium who is able to assist those who have passed on to the higher life but are still reliving the trauma of death and the process of dying, often unaware that they have died.

soul. There are many possible interpretations of this but my reference is to the individual, eternal, spiritual nature of a being which is linked to the subconscious mind or self and gives the being its own unique quality or nature; also referred to as Higher Self, Essence, Superconscious, or Spiritual Self by some. It is the "Father within" of Christ.

spirit. This also has many meanings but is often used to describe the essential or divine nature of a human being that is eternal and never dies. Many mediums use this term to describe those beings who have left the physical world and exist in the higher worlds, referring to them as "Spirit" or "Spirits," hence the term spiritualism. Some speak of visiting or communicating spirits.

trance medium. An individual who can alter their mental focus or state of consciousness, so that beings from other dimensions and non-physical worlds can operate and communicate directly through them. Usually to speak but also for other purposes such as healing, writing and in some instances painting, or playing a musical instrument.

$\mathcal{A}$ cknowledgements

As any author knows, there are many other people who play a vital role in the realisation and publishing of a book: it is always a team effort. Without the team's skills, hard work, dedication and encouragement nothing would happen, so I would like to say thank you to them hoping I have not omitted anyone.

First of all thank you to Annie Quinn who encouraged me, believed in the idea of the text, supported me and started the whole process. I am also extremely grateful for the superb editing, patience and guidance of Deborah Parker and further editing by Jean Ardell. Restructuring and making sense of my first raw manuscripts is surely a daunting task! I am also indebted to Teri Rider for bringing her many talents to the project, amongst them the producing of a superb cover design, excellent text layout and eventual publishing. Candi Sari had the tough task of proofreading, so many thanks to her, too.

I always value immensely the love, help and inspiration I continually receive in all my work from my loving family, many good friends, students and clients, especially Sue for her typing of my early indecipherable scribblings.

Then there are those particular clients who afforded me the privilege of sharing with them those intimate and often emotional contacts made with their departed loved ones. Thank you. I learned so much in those moments.

And of course not to forget the many invisible angels and friends of all types whose "visits" and messages when "looking through" at our world made this book possible. What love they reveal to us!

My heartfelt thanks are with you all.

Paul Lambillion

About the Author

Paul Lambillion is a healer, clairvoyant, teacher and lecturer who has worked in a broad range of spiritual and metaphysical fields for over 30 years. He has written many articles and several books including *Auras and Colours*, *How to Heal and Be Healed*, *Being Loving is Being Healthy*, and *Staying Cool*, several appearing in foreign editions. His self-unfoldment recordings are available from his website.

Paul has appeared on television and broadcast on radio in various countries including the UK, Ireland, the USA and South Africa. He has clients all over the world and travels widely to present courses, trainings and to counsel corporate clients and individuals in the UK, Germany, Ireland, Austria, Switzerland, Lichtenstein, the USA, and Spain.

In his earlier life he worked as a schoolmaster, fine artist, professional singer, and salesman. He currently resides in Bury St. Edmunds, Suffolk, UK and has three grown children, a granddaughter, and an affectionate, if sometimes manipulative, dog.

Paul has a great love of life, a natural talent as a communicator and is an extremely humorous teacher, having touched the lives of many thousands of people.

A note from the author

Dear Reader,

Thank you for reading my book. It was written to inform, inspire, and comfort, as well as to explain that the human individual continues to exist beyond what we call death; that those we have known and loved continue to be interested in us and our welfare, and certainly can and do seek to communicate with us should we wish them to; and that such communication is natural, benign and loving.

I hope you find it useful as you work through your own journey here on the earth, with its ups and downs, highs and lows, births and partings, and that these stories offer a glimpse along the way that there is a higher purpose to our existence, however impenetrable that purpose's meaning may seem at times.

I am always interested to hear from those who have read my books, and if it was valuable to you, do let us know. If you enjoyed it, and you have the time I'd be very grateful if you would write a review on any relevant book site to help others who might also like to read it.

Thank you once more.

Paul Lambillion

Contact Information:
www.paullambillion.co.uk
email:paul@paullambillion.co.uk.
Tel/fax 0044 (0)1284 764780

Angels Looking Through may be purchased online world-wide through Amazon and other select book retailers. To find your local independent bookseller, please visit IndieBound.org.

If you enjoyed reading *Angels Looking Through* and could spare a few moments to leave a review on Amazon, that would be incredibly helpful. Reviews are a good way for other readers to find books that may interest them. *Thank you!*

Other books by Paul Lambillion

Staying Cool
Newleaf / Gill & Macmillan, 2004

How to Heal & Be Healed
Gateway / Gill & Macmillan, 2002

Auras & Colours
Gateway / Gill & Macmillan, 2001

Communications from Heartstar
LN Fowler, 1993

Being Loving is Being Healthy
LN Fowler, 1987

Lightning Source UK Ltd.
Milton Keynes UK
UKOW01f2333200217

294854UK00004B/248/P